Visualizing Graph Data

Visualizing Graph Data

COREY L. LANUM

MANNING

SHELTER ISLAND

For online information and ordering of this and other Manning books, please visit
www.manning.com. The publisher offers discounts on this book when ordered in quantity.
For more information, please contact

> Special Sales Department
> Manning Publications Co.
> 20 Baldwin Road
> PO Box 761
> Shelter Island, NY 11964
> Email: orders@manning.com

Manning Publications Co.
20 Baldwin Road
PO Box 761
Shelter Island, NY 11964

Development editor: Cynthia Kane
Copyeditor: Linda Recktenwald
Proofreader: Katie Tennant
Technical proofreader: Pablo Dominguez Vaselli
Typesetter: Dennis Dalinnik
Illustrator: April Milne
Cover designer: Marija Tudor

ISBN: 9781617293078
Printed in the United States of America
1 2 3 4 5 6 7 8 9 10 – EBM – 21 20 19 18 17 16

brief contents

contents

preface

When I was a freshly minted college graduate, my first job saw me working as a contractor for an intelligence agency, building desktop applications in Visual Basic to connect databases to a visual front end. I've been working in this industry for almost two decades, and although the technology has changed, the problem of making sense of the relationships embedded in vast quantities of data has become even more urgent. In today's marketplace, there's a real need to be able to understand data quickly, effectively, and elegantly.

More organizations are collecting more data for more purposes every day than a team of analysts could parse in an entire career. It used to be only large government agencies that were handling this volume of data, but now even small-scale companies are gathering information on that enormous scale. Big data is no longer merely the province of government.

The biggest problem facing industry is that too much data is being collected, and most of it is irrelevant. So how do you see the trees in the forest?

Graph visualization is just one of many top-notch tools to identify patterns in this universe of big data, but it's ideally suited for aiding nonscientists to gain an understanding of what's going on in their data and to make informed decisions about how to handle it. If you're not making decisions based on the data, then why bother collecting it in the first place?

With the explosion of interest in graph databases over the past decade, visualizing data has become a powerful way to harness the potential of those databases and significantly increase their value. With today's graph visualization technology, retail websites can easily weed out fraudulent reviews, insurance agencies can pick up on suspicious claims faster, and airlines can streamline their routes. The Dutch government even uses visualizations to manage its canal system. The applications for graph data visualization are many, and as big data continues to get bigger, it's an industry with nearly unlimited growth.

I'm regularly invited to conferences across the world to speak about techniques for visualizing graphs. I was approached by Manning with a proposal to turn my lectures into book format and so share these data-harnessing ideas with a wider audience. As writing progressed, the book grew, but in the end, it became a primer on graph visualization and an introduction to some of the tools used to work with graph data. This area is a lot of fun, and the visualizations can often be aesthetically beautiful as well as useful, and I'm happy to share that with you.

In this book, I chose to highlight KeyLines and Gephi for two reasons. Gephi is a free, open source tool that's easy to use to get a quick look at your own data. Although the user interface has its warts, it's the standard for data scientists and has become more powerful with each release. As for KeyLines, I admit a bias: I'm employed by Cambridge Intelligence, the company that makes KeyLines. Nevertheless, I think it's the most powerful JavaScript library for producing graph visualizations available, and because it does only one thing, it makes explaining basic visualization concepts easy. I included an appendix to discuss D3.js because it's a powerful tool itself, although it's a bit more complex.

acknowledgments

I'd like to thank my wife, MJ, for the many late nights spent helping me edit chapters and learning more about graphs than she ever really wanted to know. For fans of her *Immersion* series of young-adult fiction, I apologize that I took her away from writing the second and third installments; please forgive me.

I'd also like to thank the team at Manning for giving me the opportunity to write this book and for patiently allowing the time to refine it into a work that I'm willing to attach my name to. In particular, my editor Cynthia Kane has provided the right mix of encouragement, constructive criticism, and well-deserved scolding for missing my deadlines—if this book doesn't match the platonic ideal represented by *Object Oriented Perl* (Damian Conway, 1999, Manning Publications), the blame falls squarely on me. Also, Pablo Domínguez Vaselli, my technical proofer, has been a huge help in ensuring that I didn't make any false statements and that my source code ran, and I'm very grateful for that help.

My appreciation also goes out to reviewers Rodrigo Candido de Abreu, John D. Lewis, Aseem Anand, Sumit Pal, Tony M. Dubitsky, David Krieff, Prof Jan Aerts, Lukasz Bonenberg, Jonathan Suever, Rocio Chongtay, and Heather Campbell for helping me to make the book the best it can be.

The team at Cambridge Intelligence has been very helpful as well. I'd like to thank my boss and the company founder, Joe Parry, for giving me the latitude to work on this book and for building a company that has been an enjoyable place to work. Marco Liberati is my JavaScript role model and has been helpful with answering many of my questions about the source code in the book, and Andrew Disney has gracefully given me permission to draw from some of his in-depth knowledge for the case studies in chapter 2.

While I was writing the early chapters of this book, my daughter Hazel was born, so *Visualizing Graph Data* is dedicated to her. Maybe she'll learn how to read from this book instead of *Where's Spot?*

about this book

This book covers graph visualization, which may sound like an incredibly niche subject but actually has broad applicability. Graphs are a helpful way of organizing data to better understand the relationships contained within that data, and visualization helps expose that organization visually. Combining the two allows people who aren't data scientists to make more sense of and understand their data. In this world of big data, it can go a long way toward giving that data some value. In the book, I discuss both basic principles of graph visualization and how to implement those principles, by examining case studies and some implementations using code.

If you're reading the printed version of this book, the figures will be in grayscale. I've checked to ensure that the images make sense in grayscale, but to see them in full color, take a look at the electronic version of this book, or download all the images from the book's website here: www.manning.com/books/visualizing-graph-data.

Who should read this book

This book is designed to be an introduction to the basic concepts of graph visualization. It contains some case studies, some technical content, and some advice, but it's not a comprehensive overview of graph theory or even graph drawing. Readers who are interested in learning about the domain, who may be data scientists or engineers, or who may be technical readers who have some data and want to understand the relationships embedded in the data will benefit from this book. It's not an academic book, and PhD graph theorists will likely find that the material is a bit too basic for them. There is some JavaScript code in this book. It's not critical to be a

JavaScript developer to find this book helpful, because the implementations using Gephi have no code. But if you want to develop web-based visualizations, some JavaScript knowledge will be required.

How this book is organized

This book is divided into two parts, with 10 chapters and an appendix. The first part stays at a high level, introducing graphs and how they can be valuable along with some case studies and a discussion of how to get your data into a graph model. Part 2 goes into more detail on how to build graph visualizations and what you need to keep in mind.

Part 1 of the book discusses graphs and graph visualization at a theoretical level—why would you want to visualize graphs and what value does it provide? I also give a brief introduction to the tools that I will be using to illustrate examples in part 2.

Chapter 1 describes the theory and history behind graph visualizations and identifies when they're an appropriate way to illustrate data.

Chapter 2 explores a mix of case studies where graph visualizations were used effectively in areas of counterterrorism, credit-card fraud, cyber security, fraudulent online reviews, and other areas in both the government and private sectors.

Chapter 3 introduces KeyLines and Gephi, the two programs most commonly used for graph visualizations (and which are referenced throughout the book).

In part 2, we dive a bit more into the details of graph visualization and how to implement specific concepts on sample data sets using KeyLines and Gephi.

Chapters 4 and 5 define the key terminology of graph visualizations and dive into tutorials that will help you draw your own graphs.

Chapters 6 and 7 teach you fancier techniques to build elegant graphs that are decluttered, interactive (with the option of using animation, 3D, and optimization for touch screens), and well laid out.

Chapter 8 troubleshoots common problems with visualizing large data sets and explains how to filter your data.

Chapter 9 investigates the best ways to visualize ever-changing data and the different options you have to graph changes to data over time.

Chapter 10 shows how to graph map data, modeling locations as a graph and overlaying graphs on a map.

The appendix gives a brief introduction to D3.js, one of the more popular visualization libraries that has some graph capabilities.

Especially in part 2, I build on concepts discussed in the previous chapters in my examples, so I suggest at least skimming the chapters in order. After that, you can go back and read the ones that are of interest to you in more detail.

About the code

This book contains some JavaScript code that shows the details of building graph visualizations in KeyLines and D3. I've made all the code publicly available on Manning's

Git server and also hosted it on a page on the Cambridge Intelligence website. The code examples use KeyLines version 3.0 (but should work for subsequent versions) and D3 version 4.

This book contains many examples of source code both in numbered listings and inline with normal text. In both cases, source code is formatted in a `fixed-width font like this` to separate it from ordinary text.

In many cases, the original source code has been reformatted; we've added line breaks and reworked indentation to accommodate the available page space in the book. In rare cases, even this was not enough, and listings include line-continuation markers (➡). In addition, comments in the source code have often been removed from the listings when the code is described in the text. Code annotations accompany many of the listings, highlighting important concepts.

Author Online

Purchase of *Visualizing Graph Data* includes free access to a private web forum run by Manning Publications, where you can make comments about the book, ask technical questions, and receive help from the author and from other users. To access the forum and subscribe to it, point your web browser at www.manning.com/books/visualizing-graph-data. This page provides information on how to get on the forum once you are registered, what kind of help is available, and the rules of conduct on the forum.

Manning's commitment to our readers is to provide a venue where a meaningful dialogue between individual readers and between readers and the author can take place. It is not a commitment to any specific amount of participation on the part of the author, whose contribution to the Author Online forum remains voluntary (and unpaid). We suggest you try asking him some challenging questions, lest his interest stray! The Author Online forum and the archives of previous discussions will be accessible from the publisher's website as long as the book is in print.

about the author

Corey Lanum is the commercial director for Cambridge Intelligence, the makers of KeyLines graph visualization software. He has nearly 20 years of experience in the realm of data analytics and visualization. When not writing technical books or building data visualizations, he is a competitive marathoner and jazz pianist. He lives in Massachusetts with his wife, two children, and dog. You can contact the author at corey.lanum@gmail.com.

about the cover illustration

The figure on the cover of *Visualizing Graph Data* is captioned "A Persian Gentleman." The illustration is taken from Thomas Jefferys' *A Collection of the Dresses of Different Nations, Ancient and Modern*, London, published between 1757 and 1772. The title page states that these are hand-colored copperplate engravings, heightened with gum arabic. Thomas Jefferys (1719–1771) was called "Geographer to King George III." He was an English cartographer who was the leading map supplier of his day. He engraved and printed maps for government and other official bodies and produced a wide range of commercial maps and atlases, especially of North America. His work as a map maker sparked an interest in local dress customs of the lands he surveyed and mapped, and which are brilliantly displayed in this four-volume collection.

Fascination with faraway lands and travel for pleasure were relatively new phenomena in the late eighteenth century, and collections such as this one were popular, introducing both the tourist as well as the armchair traveler to the inhabitants of other countries. The diversity of the drawings in Jefferys' volumes speaks vividly of the uniqueness and individuality of the world's nations some 200 years ago. Dress codes have changed since then, and the diversity by region and country, so rich at the time, has faded away. It is now often hard to tell the inhabitant of one continent from another. Perhaps, trying to view it optimistically, we have traded a cultural and visual diversity for a more varied personal life—certainly, for a more varied and interesting intellectual and technical life.

At a time when it is hard to tell one computer book from another, Manning celebrates the inventiveness and initiative of the computer business with book covers based on the rich diversity of regional life of two centuries ago, brought back to life by Jefferys' pictures.

Part 1

Graph
visualization basics

In part one of this book, we'll take a high-level view of graphs. First, I'll introduce you to what graphs are and how they can be used across a variety of domains, with some detailed case studies. Then, we'll dive a little deeper into graph models of data, how they might be different from standard relational models of data, and how you can create graph data models from your data. I'll introduce you to the two tools that we'll use throughout the book: Gephi and KeyLines. I'll use both Gephi and KeyLines in later chapters to illustrate how you can create graph visualizations of your own—for you own use, with Gephi, or as part of a visualization application, using KeyLines.

Getting to know
graph visualization

This chapter covers

- Getting to know graphs as data models
- Why graphs are a useful way to think about data
- When to visualize graphs, and the node-link drawing concept
- Other visualizations of graph data and when they're useful

In December 2001, the Enron Corporation filed for what was at the time the largest ever corporate bankruptcy. Its stock had fallen from a high of $90 per share the previous year to $0.61, decimating its employees' pensions and shareholders' investments in it. The FBI's investigation into this collapse became the largest white-collar criminal investigation in history as they seized over 3,000 boxes of documents and 4 terabytes of data. Among the information seized were about 600,000 emails between key executives at the organization. Although the FBI took pains to read every email individually, the investigators recognized that they were unlikely to find a smoking gun—people committing complex financial fraud seldom disclose their actions in written form. And in 2001, emails were only starting to become the primary means of internal communications; lots of information was still exchanged via phone calls.

In addition to looking at the text of individual emails, the FBI also wanted to uncover patterns in the communications, perhaps in an attempt to better understand who the decision makers were within Enron or who had access to a lot of the information internal to the company. To do this, they modeled the Enron emails as a *graph*.

A *graph* is a model of data that consists of *nodes*, which are discrete data elements (such as people), and *edges*, which are relationships between nodes. The graph model brings to the forefront relationships that may be hidden in tabular views of the same data and illustrates what is most important. By making those relationships between the data elements a core part of the data structure, you can identify patterns in the data that wouldn't otherwise be apparent. But building graph data structures is only half the solution to pattern recognition. This book will teach you how to visualize graphs using interactive node-link visualization diagrams, and by the end, you'll be able to create your own dynamic, interactive visualizations using a variety of tools available today.

In this chapter, I'll go a little deeper into the concept of a graph and graph history and uses, and talk about various techniques used to visualize graph data. Subsequent chapters build on this framework by introducing concrete examples of graph visualizations and the data they're based on and discuss various techniques for creating useful visualizations.

1.1 Getting to know graphs

Graphs are everywhere. As long as you're interested in how items can be related to each other, there's a graph somewhere in your data. In this section, I'll walk you through what a graph is and what can be gained from visualizing graphs.

1.1.1 What is a graph?

As described previously, a graph—also called a *network*—is a set of interconnected data elements that's expressed as a series of nodes and edges.

In the common definition of a graph, edges have exactly two endpoints, no more. In some cases, those two endpoints can be the same node if a node links to itself. An edge (also known as a link) can take one of two forms:

- *Directed*—The relationship has a direction. Stella owns the car, but it doesn't make sense to say the car owns Stella.
- *Undirected*—The two items are linked without the concept of direction; the relationship inherently goes both ways. If Stella is linked to Roger because they committed a crime together, it means the same thing to say Stella was arrested with Roger as it does to say Roger was arrested with Stella.

In figure 1.1, you see an example of a directed link with properties.

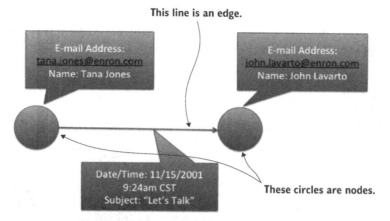

Figure 1.1 A property graph of a single email between Enron executives. The two nodes are the sender and recipient of the email, and the directed edge is the email.

Both nodes and edges can have *properties*, which are key-value pairs—lists of properties and values, describing either the data element itself or the relationship. Figure 1.2 is a simple property graph showing that Stella bought a 2008 Volkswagen Jetta in September 2007 and sold it in October 2013. Modeling it as a graph highlights that Stella had a relationship with this car, albeit temporarily.

An email is a relationship, too, between the sender and the recipient. The properties of the nodes are things like email address, name, and title, and the properties of the relationship are the date/time it was sent, its subject line, and the text of the email.

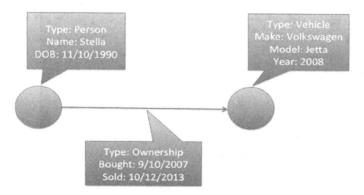

Figure 1.2 A simple property graph with two nodes and an edge. Stella (the first node) bought a 2008 Volkswagen Jetta (the second node) in September 2007 and sold it in October 2013. Modeling it as a graph highlights that Stella had a relationship with this car (the edge).

To prove conspiracy, the FBI was interested in all the emails sent among the Enron executives, not just a single one, so let's add some more nodes to represent a larger number of emails sent during a specified period of time, as shown in figure 1.3.

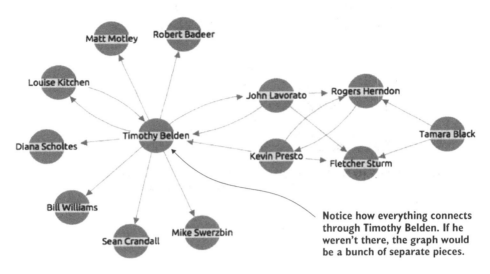

Notice how everything connects through **Timothy Belden**. If he weren't there, the graph would be a bunch of separate pieces.

Figure 1.3   A graph of some of the Enron executives' email communications. You can easily see that Timothy Belden is a hub of communication in this segment of Enron, sending and receiving email from many other executives.

Figure 1.3 is a *directed graph* because it matters whether Kevin Presto sent an email to Timothy Belden or received one—there's a big difference between sending and receiving information when you're investigating who knew what when. The arrowheads on the edges show that directionality: Kevin Presto sent an email to Timothy Belden, but Timothy Belden didn't reply, indicating they may not have been close associates or they may have spoken offline. As we start to add more data to the graph, you can see the value of graphs—patterns become apparent. In this example, we can easily see that Timothy Belden is a hub of communication in this segment of Enron, sending and receiving email from many other executives.

1.1.2   *A bit of theory*

Graph theory began early in the eighteenth century with the Seven Bridges of Königsberg problem. In Königsberg, Prussia (now Kaliningrad, Russia), it was a common parlor game to try to determine a route that would allow someone to pass over all seven bridges over the Pregel River exactly once without passing over any bridge twice. (Go ahead and give it a shot using the map of the city, shown in figure 1.4, and see if you can prove three centuries of mathematicians wrong.)

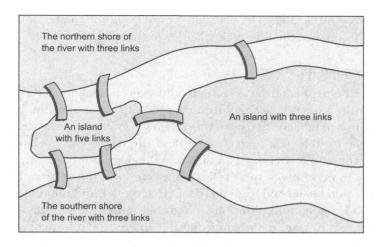

Figure 1.4 The Seven Bridges of Königsberg problem. Using this map of the bridges of Königsberg, Prussia, try to draw a route that reaches each area of the city but never crosses the same bridge twice.

Leonhard Euler proved this problem unsolvable by abstracting the regions of the city into individual points and the bridges as paths between those points, as you can see in figure 1.5.

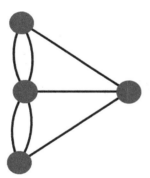

Figure 1.5 Seven bridges and four land areas of Königsberg as a graph. In this graph, nodes denote the land masses bordering the Pregel River and the two islands in its middle. Edges represent the bridges connecting the two islands and two shorelines.

Each land area of Königsberg is indicated by a point, and the bridges are the lines that connect the points. This is a graph, just like the Enron graph. The graph model in figure 1.5 makes it easier to see that nodes with an even number of links can be navigated easily (you can enter and exit using two different links), but nodes with an odd number of links can only be either the beginning or the end of a path (this is obvious for a node with only one link, but you can also see it applies to three, five, and so on). The number of links from a node is called that node's *degree*. The Königsberg bridge problem can now be proven solvable only if at most two nodes have odd degrees and the rest have even degrees. This diagram doesn't satisfy that condition, and therefore it's impossible to cross each bridge only once; so graph theory has answered a problem previously considered intractable. The principle of nodes with even and odd degrees applies to all graphs, not just the Königsberg bridge problem.

1.1.3   *Introducing the graph data model*

Graphs are interesting mathematical constructs, and many academic mathematicians have spent their entire careers studying the domain. But the purpose of this book is to describe how graphs can be derived from data and how they can be presented to nonmathematicians so that they can better understand the data. Let's go back to the Enron example. I chose to model the data such that the nodes were the employees at Enron and the emails were represented as links between them, but that's not the only graph model that could be derived from this data. That model, and the resulting visualization, shows who is communicating with whom but ignores basic data about the email itself. And it fails to take into account possible interesting information such as forwarding of emails or sending a single email to multiple people, some of whom may be CC'd or BCC'd.

> **DEFINITION**   A *visualization* is any method of using imagery to convey a point. With relation to computer graphics, it typically means finding a way to show large amounts of data in a single view. Creating images to show graph data is called *graph visualization.*

In this case, you may want to consider the email itself a node. Figure 1.6 shows the sender and the recipients of an email with the subject line "Let's Talk," sent among Enron executives. The nodes are executives from Enron, and the edges represent how they received the email (whether they were in the To:, CC:, or BCC: fields).

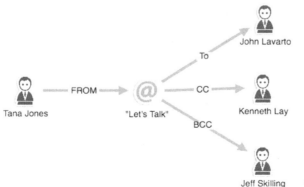

Figure 1.6   **Graphing a single email at Enron**

Consider the following very simple table. Table 1.1 consists of only two columns: a list of names and the countries where those names are used. In the United States, the Social Security Administration releases a similar table each year showing the popularity of first names given to babies, as measured by new applications for Social Security numbers.

Table 1.1 A list of names and countries where those names are common

Name	Country
Joe	United States
Juan	Mexico
João	Brazil
Jean	France
Antoine	France
Jean	United States
Ignacio	Mexico
João	Portugal

This can be modeled as a graph—show each name as a node and each country as a node. A link between name and country nodes exists if the name and country appear in the same row. The result looks like figure 1.7.

Figure 1.7 Using a graph to illustrate a table of name/country pairs

This graph tells us more than is immediately obvious from the table, namely, that *Jean* is used both in France and the United States. It also shows that *João* is used in Brazil and Portugal, but no other names are associated with those countries. As you can see, you can generate graph models from even the simplest data set, but typically you're going to want properties on the nodes, the links, or both. In this case, you may want the frequency of a name's use in a country as a property of the link and perhaps whether that name is typically used by males or females.

1.1.4 When are graphs helpful?

Now that you understand what graphs are, why would you use them? Although there are certainly cases where a graph model wouldn't be appropriate—a long key-value pairing comes to mind—they can be very useful when there are relationships between your data elements. If the nodes are connected to one another somehow, and those connections are as important as the data itself, then a graph is a useful model for understanding the data. For example, in a list of financial data, it may be important to look at the data in aggregate, say in a budget where you're interested in the total amount spent in a set of categories. A graph would be counterproductive in this instance, because you aren't looking for connections within this data. You care only about the bottom line. But in the same set of data, if you're interested in the transactions embedded in the data—for example, which consumers are spending money at which merchants, and which merchants are using which banks—then a graph would be a very useful model for storing and visualizing that data.

VALUE OF GRAPHS

Graphs can be incredibly useful, but there's a danger in overusing them. Many people, when first exposed to graph concepts, begin to see graphs everywhere, in every data set, but a graph can sometimes obscure the meaning of the data.

Graphs are a good choice in the following situations:

- *The links between items are not obvious.* For example, linking someone's first name and last name together is unlikely to be useful unless you're looking at the relationship of the names when they are independent of each other. "How many 'Coreys' drive black cars?"
- *There's a structure embedded in the data.* If every link has unique end points with no other links, then the graph is a bunch of disconnected links that doesn't answer any interesting question.
- *There are at least some properties on the nodes.* If a data set doesn't have any properties, then it may create a pretty picture when drawn, but it's impossible to tell what you're looking at.

Figure 1.8 shows a graph model that's not very helpful. It represents the data found in the back of a road atlas that shows the mileage and driving times between city pairs.

In reality, every city in North America is connected to every other city via roads, and it's unlikely that the atlas browser wants to bother adding up the various segments and city pairs necessary to drive from Richmond to Buffalo; they just want to know how far it is and how long it takes to get there. In this case, they might prefer an association matrix, which is a different way of representing graphs.

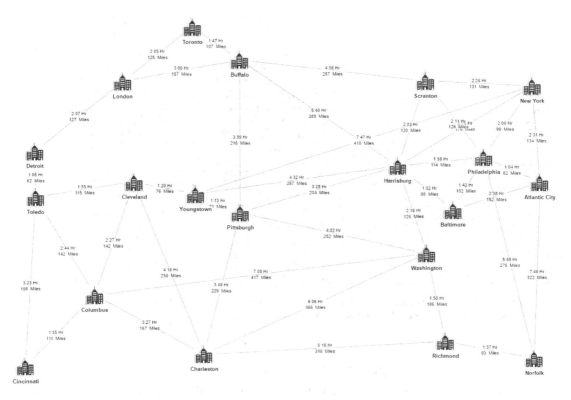

Figure 1.8 A graph of driving times between North American cities. A graph is not an effective way of presenting this type of data because in reality everything is connected to everything else.

ASSOCIATION MATRIX An association matrix is a table displaying the node names as both columns and rows. For each pair of nodes that has a link between them, the cell of intersection is either marked or filled in with a property value. In an undirected graph, the values will be repeated, because each node pairing appears twice: once with the first node as a row and the second as a column, and then vice versa.

The table shown in figure 1.9 is an association matrix presenting similar data on the distance between city pairs.

Sets of data where the relationships between the data elements are the most important feature are the most useful to model as a graph. Graphs work best when you have a key component of analysis. In this section, you've had a brief introduction to the graph data model, how tabular data can be represented as a graph (in section 1.1.3, "Introducing the graph data model"), and when graphs might be useful. In the next section, we'll discuss how and when to visualize graphs, that is, draw pictures of this data model on paper or on computer screens.

	Atlanta	Boston	Chicago	Dallas	Denver	Houston	Las Vegas	Los Angeles	Miami	New Orleans	New York	Phoenix	San Francisco	Seattle	Washington D.C.
Atlanta		1095	715	805	1437	844	1920	2230	675	499	884	1832	2537	2730	657
Boston	1095		983	1815	1991	1886	2500	3036	1539	1541	213	2664	3179	3043	440
Chicago	715	983		931	1050	1092	1500	2112	1390	947	840	1729	2212	2052	695
Dallas	805	1815	931		801	242	1150	1425	1332	504	1604	1027	1765	2122	1372
Denver	1437	1991	1050	801		1032	885	1174	2094	1305	1780	836	1266	1373	1635
Houston	844	1886	1092	242	1032		1525	1556	1237	365	1675	1158	1958	2348	1443
Las Vegas	1920	2500	1500	1150	885	1525		289	2640	1805	2486	294	573	1188	2568
Los Angeles	2230	3036	2112	1425	1174	1556	289		2757	1921	2825	398	403	1150	2680
Miami	675	1539	1390	1332	2094	1237	2640	2757		892	1328	2359	3097	3389	1101
New Orleans	499	1541	947	504	1305	365	1805	1921	892		1330	1523	2269	2626	1098
New York	884	213	840	1604	1780	1675	2486	2825	1328	1330		2442	3036	2900	229
Phoenix	1832	2664	1729	1027	836	1158	294	398	2359	1523	2442		800	1482	2278
San Francisco	2537	3179	2212	1765	1266	1958	573	403	3097	2269	3036	800		817	2864
Seattle	2730	3043	2052	2122	1373	2348	1188	1150	3389	2626	2900	1482	817		2755
Washington D.C.	657	440	695	1372	1635	1443	2568	2680	1101	1098	229	2278	2864	2755	

Figure 1.9   The back page of a road atlas. City names are represented as both columns and rows, and the cell of intersection indicates the distance between them.

1.2   *Getting to know graph visualization*

Why does visualizing graph data make it easier to understand? There are two reasons. Humans are intuitively visual creatures, and it's almost impossible to think of a model—any sort of model—and not picture how it looks. Ernest Rutherford developed the model of the atom in 1909 that we're all familiar with, a nucleus of protons and neutrons with electrons whizzing in orbits around the nucleus. This model was quickly replaced by Erwin Schrodinger's more accurate model based on quantum mechanics, but Rutherford's model is still, 90 years later, the one that the public embraces. Why? Because it can be pictured. The Schrodinger model is more accurate, but it's a mathematical concept, not a visual one, and therefore has never acquired broad public appeal. Data is the same way; unless we can show our audience what we're talking about, they won't recall it. Visualization helps bridge that gap and allows the decision-makers to understand the data.

I described the property graph model, with nodes, edges, and properties, in section 1.1, but the topic of this book is graph visualization. The sole reason for data collection is to make better-informed decisions based on the data, so it's important to provide a useful way of accessing it. And with graph data, that typically means drawing the graph.

Although there are many different methods of graph visualization, and I'll briefly discuss some of them, the focus of this book is on node-link visualization. This is not to say that other visualizations are never useful, but node-link visualizations tend to have the broadest appeal regardless of the data source and require the least amount of technical knowledge to understand. I've been using node-link visualization so far in this chapter, and it's just what it sounds like. Nodes are points or polygons or icons, and links are lines connecting those points. Node-link diagrams are almost always drawn on a 2D plane and almost never three-dimensional. An important aspect of the node-link diagram is that a node's location doesn't tell you anything interesting about that node, although there are different ways of positioning nodes that can reveal some useful information based on location. Nodes are placed solely for convenience and readability, which makes this quite different from a Cartesian scatter plot, for example. An effect of this is that layout, or how nodes are arranged on the chart, becomes much more important. Two charts with identical data but different layouts can imply different things to the human eye.

1.2.1 When to visualize graphs

There are two reasons to visualize graphs, both of which are important:

- The first is to better understand the structure of the data that you have.
- The second purpose of visualization is to expose a broader audience to the data connections.

VISUALIZING GRAPH DATA STRUCTURE

The visualization in figure 1.10 shows the structure of the sales database and how its elements are connected to each other, but not the connections between individual employees and products.

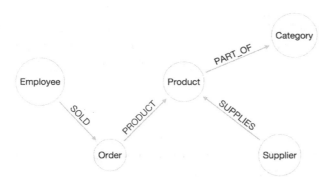

Figure 1.10 A sales database showing connections between different data types

With regard to the first purpose, understanding the structure: in a data set, what sorts of things are linked to other things? Many of the diagrams you'll see from graph databases are designed to illuminate this structure.

In this example, the structure of a sales database is visualized. Suppliers supply products that are members of categories. Employees take orders that consist of products. To a data scientist or an application engineer, this view is very important; it helps define the model of the data, how it's stored, and how users will interact with it. Get this wrong, and it can be a very time-consuming and expensive process to fix.

DRAWING YOUR GRAPH DATA

The second purpose is to visualize the data inside your data set. In this case, you're not interested in the categories of data but the actual relationships among the data elements themselves. Instead of saying "Employees sell orders that consist of products," you can get specific and say "Brad from Home Depot sold me a Husqvarna chainsaw." Then you can get more specific—who else is buying Husqvarna chainsaws from Home Depot? What other products are included in those orders? The visualization allows you to better understand the connections embedded within the data itself.

A key reason that graph visualization is important is it gives a visual interface to data discovery. Although much of the big data revolution of the past decade has been in understanding trends in the aggregate data, it's equally important to discover previously unknown connections and relationships between the individual data elements. A dashboard will be unlikely to show this, but a graph will allow the user to explore the data and discover these patterns visually. I'll discuss this more in chapter 6.

1.2.2 *Alternative graph visualizations*

The node-link visualization isn't the only way to display a graph, although it's the main focus of this book. In section 1.1, I mentioned the association matrix, where nodes are represented by columns and rows, and a mark (or a value) in the cell shows that there's a relationship between those two nodes. The road atlas in figure 1.9 is a good example. I find the association matrix very useful for creating or editing graph data, but not as helpful for explaining it to others. Next, I'll show you some examples of visualizations that are better than node-link visualizations for certain types of data.

CIRCLE PLOT

If the primary goal is to show aggregate links from groups of nodes, as opposed to individual data, something like the *circle plot* may make more sense. A good example is found at http://www.global-migration.info, which shows global migration between and within the six populated continents; see figure 1.11. Their data is a graph of migration patterns from each country to each other country, but a node-link diagram of all this data would be busy and wouldn't show aggregate patterns as well as the circle plot, so it was a good choice.

Figure 1.11 A graph from www.global-migration.info/. This stylish graph illustrates migration patterns among people from all six inhabited continents.

HIVE PLOT

Another example of an alternative to the node-link diagram is the *hive plot*, shown in figure 1.12. As mentioned earlier, node-link graph visualizations focus on individual data elements and the connections among them. While useful, they can fail to identify and communicate connections among different types or groups of data elements. The hive plot can be especially useful when trying to understand structure in very large networks, in tens or hundreds of thousands of nodes or links, because it differentiates nodes into three or more types and aligns them from the center of the chart on an

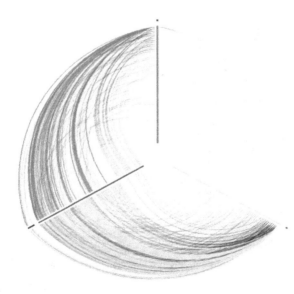

Figure 1.12 Hive plot of E. coli bacteria at http://www.hiveplot.net by Martin Krzywinski. Notice the large number of connections of the leftmost group but the fewer connections between the top and right.

axis. Links between elements of different types are drawn as curved lines around the center of the chart. This can allow a viewer to visually differentiate between two types that are tightly linked versus those that are weakly linked. It doesn't display links between elements in the same type and makes a drill-down, to look at subsets of the data, much more difficult.

There are many benefits to using node-link diagrams to better understand data, but at other times other visualizations are more helpful. In general, node-links are valuable when you want to focus on specifics, and are less helpful when you're interested in aggregates, as you just saw.

SANKEY DIAGRAM

Another useful visualization is the Sankey diagram, which is designed to plot flows of something (money, people, energy, and so on) from left to right in the chart. With traditional graph data, you're most interested in the relationship between the two nodes and any properties of that relationship, but a Sankey diagram is designed to highlight aggregate amounts between categories of nodes. The example in figure 1.13, from the International Energy Agency (https://www.iea.org/), shows the world's energy usage from raw materials on the left to consumed energy in the form of electricity or fuel on the right, with the intermediate steps in between. A node-link visualization would show individual gasoline refineries linked to individual oil fields as inputs and linked to individual gasoline wholesalers as outputs, but that's irrelevant detail if you're ultimately interested in the proportion of energy derived from various sources. The

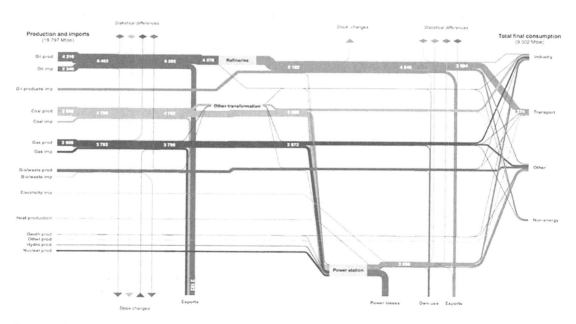

Figure 1.13   A Sankey diagram showing world energy consumption and the sources. See www.iea.org/Sankey for the larger view.

Sankey diagram makes clear what proportion of refined oil goes to transportation fuel versus electricity generation versus plastics, something that would be hard to see in a more traditional node-link visualization.

1.3 Summary

In this chapter, I introduced you to the definition of a graph and discussed the benefits of thinking about data in terms of nodes and links. I also emphasized when this is beneficial and when you'd see more benefit from a tabular view of data. I also touched on the history of graph visualization and the reasons why drawing a picture of your data can be enlightening. Although most of this book focuses on node-link visualizations, I mentioned a few other styles of visualization that can be helpful in certain circumstances.

- A graph is a model of data emphasizing the connections in the data.
- The graph model can be created from any data set where items share a common property. Some are more useful than others.
- Graph data can come from any source, not solely graph databases.
- The node-link diagram is the most common way of presenting and communicating graph data.
- Graph visualization can serve two purposes: it allows you to explore data and expose connections, and helps you communicate data connection findings to others.
- There are many other ways of displaying graph data that don't rely on the node-link diagram. Most of them help with looking at the structure of larger networks and not finer details.

Case studies

This chapter covers

- Intelligence and law enforcement graphs
- Financial and online review fraud graphs
- Cyber security
- Sales and marketing graphs

Over the past dozen years, interest in graphs has exploded beyond academia and into industry. The intelligence failures that allowed the September 11, 2001, attacks were portrayed in the media as a "failure to connect the dots" because individual government agencies had suspicions about individual terrorists, but no one was collecting and analyzing the big picture. *Connecting the dots* means understanding the relationships among individual data sets, and although it still has a lot of room for improvement, the US intelligence community was one of the first adopters of graph visualization, specifically among antiterrorism analysts and investigators. The application of graphs to interpret flows across a network also appealed to the investigators looking at money laundering. Often, discovering money laundering involves looking at financial flows among people and companies and identifying areas that don't make sense, either because they have more inflows than outflows or because they appear central in a network when they shouldn't be. Fraud isn't limited to financial fraud—any sort of misrepresentation for gain is fraud, and a relatively recent fraudulent practice is review fraud: submitting fake positive reviews of products or services in which one has a financial stake or submitting fake negative reviews of one's competitors.

Because an increasing sector of the economy is composed of these middlemen who match services or products and their customers (think OpenTable for restaurants, Uber for taxicabs, or Yelp for local businesses), the need to ensure the integrity of these reviews is critical.

I've been using *networks* thus far in the book in the generic mathematical sense, to mean any collection of nodes and the edges connecting them. Most people, however, think of a computer network either as a basic local area network or something as complex as the global internet. As the world continues to evolve toward the internet being the primary communications infrastructure, not just for people but for devices as well (the internet of things, or IoT), understanding how all these things may be connected to each other becomes increasingly important. Cyber security has become tremendously important over the last few years, as more critical functions of businesses and individuals are conducted over the internet. Graphs can be used both to identify weaknesses in computer network infrastructure and to visualize a cyber attack to determine how to stop one in progress or prevent a future one.

We'll look at all these examples in this chapter, including how graph visualizations aid law enforcement investigations at both the national and local levels and help businesses weed out fraudulent behavior by their customers or online reviewers. These case studies illustrate several different ways graph visualization has been used successfully in real life.

Table 2.1 lists some other industries where graph visualization may be useful.

Table 2.1 More industries and data where graph visualization can be used

Healthcare	Drug combination responses
	Communicable disease infection patterns
Transportation	Airline route networks
	Shipping logistics
Supply chain management	Vendor relationships
Business intelligence	Consumer buying behavior
	Consumer sentiment analysis
	Organizational analysis

The data from each of these case studies is real-life data from the domains, but some of it has been anonymized to protect confidentiality. I encourage you to download it from this book's website (www.manning.com/books/visualizing-graph-data) and play with the visualizations yourself.

2.1   *Intelligence and terrorism*

In 2004, Marc Sageman, a senior fellow at the Foreign Policy Research Institute and former CIA agent, published the book *Understanding Terror Networks*, which includes detailed biographical profiles of 172 Al Qaeda members and sympathizers across the globe and the social bonds between individuals in this group. We can understand this data as a graph by modeling the people as nodes and the relationships as edges. Let's look at a small sample of this data in tabular form, with the table in figure 2.1 supplying the people/nodes.

Name ▼	City ▼	Country ▼
Mohammed Mansour Jabarah	St. Catherine's, Ontario	Canada
Encep Nurjaman	Kampung Sungai Manggis	Malaysia
Joseph "Jihad Jack" Terrence Thomas	Melbourne, Victoria	Australia
Ali Amrozi bin Haji Nurhasyim	Tenggulun	Indonesia
Hasyim bin Abbas	Singapore	Singapore

Figure 2.1   Table of Al Qaeda members and international sympathizers and their whereabouts, taken from Marc Sageman's book *Understanding Terror Networks*. In a graph visualization, these people form the nodes.

And figure 2.2 shows the edges/relationships between these people as a matrix.

Now we'll expand this to represent all 172 terrorists in a node-link visualization, using the fact that two people know one another as a link between them in the chart. I've made a couple of design choices here; one is to use the flag of the country that the person lives in (or lived in; this is 2004 data) as the node icon. This is helpful because it allows us to tell at a glance where people are from. We'll draw all links identically. Normally, we'd want to use visual properties of the links like width and color to indicate something substantive about the data, but this data just includes whether a link exists, without a lot of properties on those links. We'll also run a force-directed

	Mohammed Masour Jabarah	Encep Nurjaman	Joseph "Jihad Jack" Terrence Thomas	Ali Amrozi bin Haji Nurhasyim	Hasyim bin Abbas
Mohammed Masour Jabarah		Knows			
Encep Nurjaman	Knows		Knows	Knows	
Joseph "Jihad Jack" Terrence Thomas		Knows		Knows	
Ali Amrozi bin Haji Nurhasyim		Knows	Knows		Knows
Hasyim bin Abbas	·			Knows	

Figure 2.2   Matrix of Al Qaeda members and international sympathizers. These relationships are represented by edges in a graph visualization.

layout, which creates separation between the nodes and attempts to make the chart more readable. I'll go into this layout in detail in chapter 7. The result is shown in figure 2.3.

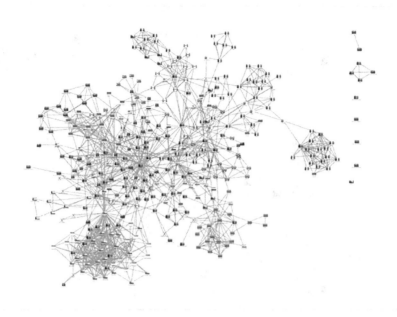

Figure 2.3 A graph visualization of Al Qaeda members and international sympathizers. Nodes are people, and edges show who knows whom.

Although we can see some of the most central nodes and isolated groups in this view, there's too much clutter to learn much at this level. There's a temptation in graph visualizations to show more and more data all at once, and that can be counterproductive, because your diagram becomes less and less readable. Zooming in on subsections of the chart can give some better insights, as shown in figure 2.4.

Now we see Encep Nurjaman, from the previous table, represented by a Malaysian flag, as the key connection point among a group of mostly Malaysians below and a mix of countries above. And this is true: Nurjaman was known as the Osama bin Laden of Southeast Asia and was the main link between Al Qaeda's Middle East arm and its Southeast Asian operations, so even with no additional information other than who knows whom, we've identified some key people in this network.

Thus, even without diving in deeper with more properties for each node, the graph visualization helps identify who knows whom on an international scale. Merely displaying the data graphically enables us to identify key patterns from a data set that would be impossible to see in tabular form. From there, we can start to look for

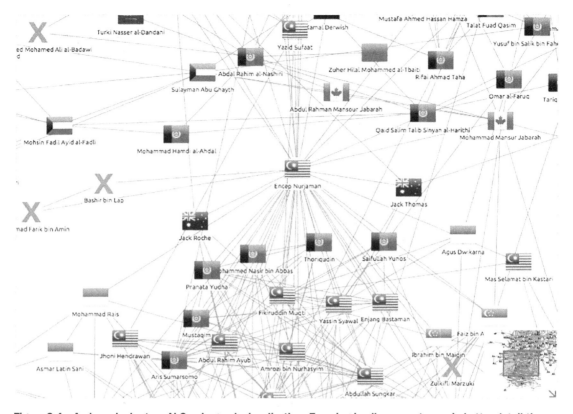

Figure 2.4   A closer look at an Al Qaeda graph visualization. Zooming in allows you to see in better detail the relationships among Encep Nurjaman, a Malaysian member of Al Qaeda, and an international group of his associates.

hubs—focal points where one cluster meets another, indicating someone with broad reach within a network.

GRAPHICAL REPRESENTATION allows you to see the most-well-connected nodes easily. Even when there's too much data in the data set to see each individual data endpoint, the patterns can still be helpful—which groups are tightly connected with lots of connections between them and which are isolated endpoints.

Let's do some basic social network analysis (SNA) to see what else we can learn.

SNA is a research field that aims to use analytic algorithms to understand social dynamics within groups. This diverse field is worthy of its own book, so we'll only touch on a few algorithms here. Our goal, as intelligence analysts, is to determine the key players in this network—who is the most central figure in Al Qaeda? SNA has a set of algorithms called *centrality scores*, which are different ways of looking at the pattern of links embedded in the data to determine which nodes are the most important. There are different ways of measuring this. One way is called *betweenness*, which looks at how much of the network flows through a particular node.

BETWEENNESS is a social network analysis centrality algorithm that assigns a score to each node. It works by calculating the shortest path (either by number of links or by a weighted value on each link) between every node and every other node on the chart. Each time a node falls on that shortest path, its betweenness score is increased. As a result, items with a high betweenness score tend to be choke points or funnels of data as it flows across the chart.

By calculating the path that comprises the fewest number of links from each node to each other node, we can determine which nodes are most often on those paths. Those nodes would get a higher betweenness score. In the chart shown in figure 2.5, we've sized the node and used the alpha (graying out) of nodes based on their betweenness score. We can clearly see Osama bin Laden in the center with the largest node (remember, this data was published in 2004) and our friend Nurjaman over on the left. There are a few other key players whose names you may recognize who stand out in this network. This is an unusual result. Betweenness doesn't typically identify the leader of an organization, because it's rare that the leader would build a network where all communications had to go through them. It's more often the case that people

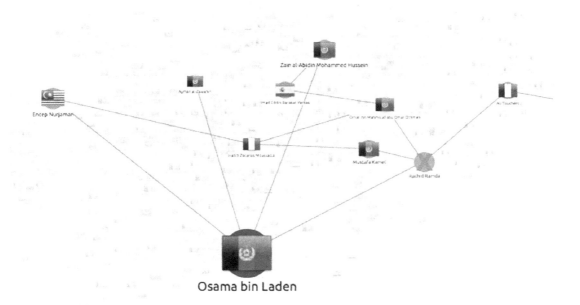

Figure 2.5 Using social network analysis to identify key players in Al Qaeda. As the leader of Al Qaeda, Osama bin Laden has the highest betweenness score in the organization, so his node is the largest in the visualization.

with the highest betweenness scores act as brokers of information as it flows across the network. So the fact that bin Laden has the highest betweenness score is interesting. He's either built a network where he is the key broker of information or, less likely, he's not the actual leader.

Another important feature of this visualization is the ability to filter. As shown in figures 2.2–2.5, it's not always helpful to look at all the nodes and links at the same time; it's often too much to make sense of. So a useful capability is one that allows us to control the visibility of nodes based on some criteria. Because we're looking at countries here, let's add the ability to filter the terrorists in our visualization based on whether they live in selected countries. Maybe instead of the Middle East or Asia, today we want to focus on Western Europe. We can use the same data to look only at the relationships between British and French terrorists and see something interesting, as shown in figure 2.6.

The networks barely overlap one another. There's one Frenchman working with the Brits in the upper left and one Brit as part of a French network in the center, but other than that, the terrorist cells are operating completely independently, at least given the information we have.

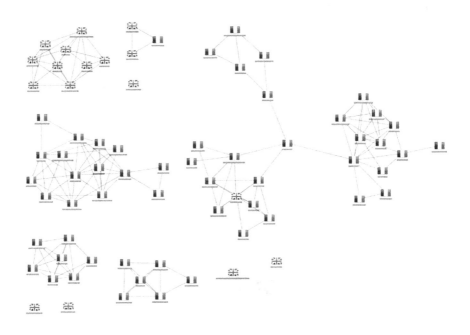

Figure 2.6   Using a filter to display only French and British members of Al Qaeda shows that members from the two countries rarely work together, with only two exceptions.

It's easy to be an armchair intelligence analyst, and this example may seem simplistic when all the data came from a single book, but understanding these types of networks can literally be a matter of life and death for soldiers in the field, and the data is rarely so well encapsulated and in a single location. It's not surprising that graph visualization is a quick and easy way for analysts to understand and communicate about large sets of complex data effectively.

Graph visualization has become an invaluable tool for law enforcement when investigating organized crime with large social networks. But a graph visualization like the one in this case study would be useful in identifying patterns of communication in any network of people, not just among criminals. Marketers also can benefit from this same technique.

2.2 *Credit card fraud*

Fraud is defined as "misrepresentation for financial gain," or basically lying to get what you want. Regardless of the type of fraud—whether it's an account takeover, where the fraudster impersonates an account owner and directs funds toward oneself, or identity theft, where a fraudster applies for credit in someone else's name or makes false insurance claims—nearly all cases of fraud involve the fabrication of a relationship. So graphs, and specifically graph visualizations, have important roles to play in combating fraud.

Graph visualization can play two roles in combating fraud; it can be useful in both *fraud detection* and *fraud investigation.*

Fraud detection is critically important. Because transactional systems have become increasingly automated over the last few decades, there are fewer human eyes to catch anomalies. In many large-scale transaction systems, such as credit card purchases, the vast majority of transactions are never reviewed by a person at all. This is generally good; it allows for immediate approval and low fees when using credit cards, but it also opens a wide door for potential fraud. Because nobody is reviewing and approving or denying transactions, as long as fraudsters stay under the radar and don't raise any alarms, they can get away with siphoning large amounts of money toward themselves. This raises the costs to all the legitimate users of the system. Companies have invested billions of dollars in automated analytics to help detect anomalous behavior in these large systems, and they do a commendable job, but some borderline cases are still reviewed by human fraud experts. This is where graph visualization comes in. These experts often have to decide dozens or even hundreds of cases per day and have little information on which to base their decisions. A quick view of data relationships can often make the difference between a correct detection of fraud, the denial of a legitimate transaction, or the inadvertent approval of an actual case of fraud.

In this section, I'll review how businesses identify fraudulent purchases using graph visualization and what specific patterns suggest fraud.

2.2.1   *The markers of online shopping fraud*

When I (or any other non-criminal) order goods from an online merchant, the graph representation of my purchase is quite trivial and might resemble the diagram shown in figure 2.7.

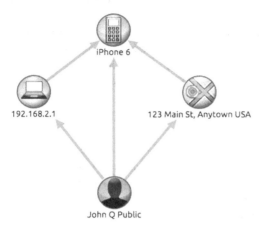

Figure 2.7   **The anatomy of an online purchase. The nodes in this graph are the customer, the product, the IP address, and the shipping address. Nothing in this transaction suggests that the purchase was made fraudulently.**

Although I may order from a number of IP addresses, perhaps my work and home computers, it's generally a small number. And the same is true with ship-to addresses. I might have items shipped to a small number of addresses, but it's unlikely to be more than a few, and they would most likely be in the same country. This gives a visual pattern to expected normal transactions and makes it easy to visually pick out graphs that don't match that pattern. For example, why is a single IP address processing orders from dozens of different accounts? Or why is a single account responsible for shipping goods to dozens of addresses in different countries from the account owner? The chart in figure 2.8 shows how fraudulent transactions stand out when visualized graphically.

Once a case of fraud has been detected, however, it's equally important to determine the scope of fraud. Is this a systemic pattern of organized criminals or a lone individual who just thought they could get away with something? How do we drill down to the source? This is called *fraud investigation*, and graph visualization can be helpful here too. Take a stolen credit card number again as an example. A cardholder recognizes a fraudulent charge on their statement and reports this to the credit card company. We've identified one case of obvious fraud and put a stop to it, but how can we use that data to proactively determine who else might be at risk? One way is to visualize the network of cardholders who have reported fraud and the merchants they have frequented. Commonalities such as the one in figure 2.9 would raise a big red flag.

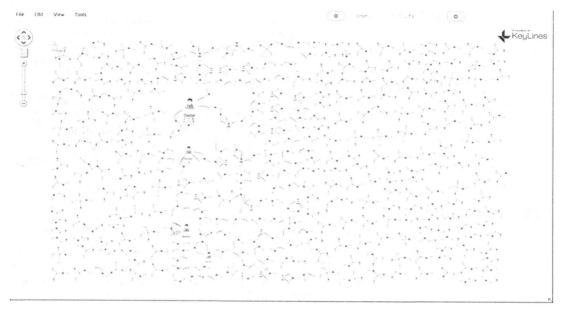

Figure 2.8 Note the similar patterns of most of the nodes, with the exception of two or three well-connected clusters near the center.

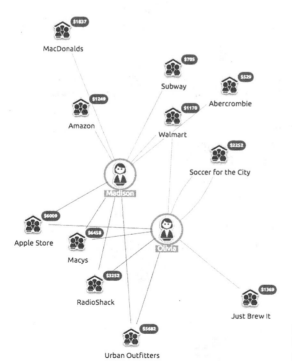

Figure 2.9 Red links show disputed transactions from these cardholders at these merchants.

Multiple victims visited the same vendors before their cards started showing fraudulent transactions; maybe one of those vendors has something to do with it. Unscrupulous employees have been known to scan customers' cards in a second, unauthorized card reader before processing a legitimate transaction and then sell the numbers on the black market. Moreover, because these transactions all took place on Tuesdays or Thursdays between 12 p.m. and 8 p.m., perhaps we can cross-reference the store's employee shift records to determine who specifically is responsible, all from graph visualization.

Merchants can use graph visualization to identify atypical shopping behaviors among their customers, which may be suggestive of fraud, before they fulfill fraudulent orders. Graphs are also useful for law enforcement in analyzing consumer behavior and tracking down perpetrators.

2.2.2   *Online review fraud*

In April 2015, Amazon filed its first-ever lawsuit over fake product reviews written by third-party companies contracted by its merchants. It alleges that an entire "unhealthy ecosystem" has developed to falsely inflate the rankings of certain products on the Amazon sales platform. Many sites that match customers to products or services add value by providing reviews, ostensibly from legitimate customers with real experience with those products or services. On Yelp, for example, it has been found that adding a single star to the score of an average business will increase sales of its products by 19%, thus creating a huge incentive for the providers to improve their ratings by any means necessary. Many of those means are legitimate—one way to improve a review score is to offer a better product or customer service—but there are illegitimate ways to inflate a ranking as well, such as paying for reviews.

As we saw in the credit card case, in addition to business owners who work to falsely inflate their own rankings and perhaps also deflate the rankings of their competitors, there are occasionally systemic fraudsters, those who exploit weaknesses in the websites' systems to manipulate scores for many of their clients, the business owners. The first group is often easy to catch because they're unsophisticated. Graph visualization makes it easy to identify, for example, a new user who creates an account, reviews seven different Italian restaurants in Phoenix, gives six of them one star and the remaining one a glowing five-star review, but the consultants are often more subtle.

A key difference between review fraud and financial fraud is that review websites don't always ask for verifiable information, such as an address or credit card number. This increases the number of reviews submitted but also makes it impossible to cross-check reviews against a watch list. Instead, we're dependent on device data, location data, and behavioral patterns, such as the following:

- Review text
- Review submission velocity
- Device fingerprints
- Profile data
- Geolocation data

2.2.3 *Visualizing review fraud*

The chart in figure 2.10 uses mock data to show a number of reviews, submitted over a two-day period, about a single business. Note that we're also interested in when these reviews happened, so we're looking at histograms that show us volume trends over time. We'll discuss this more in chapter 9.

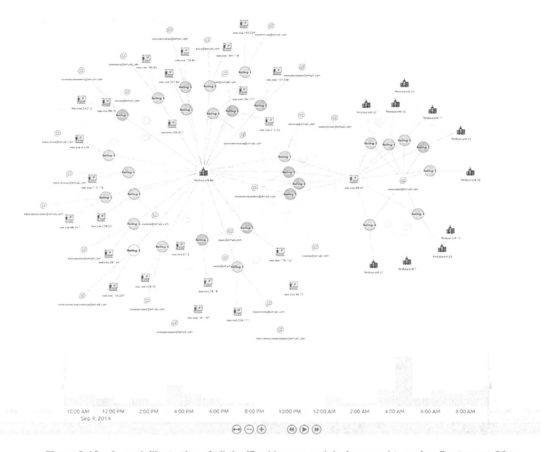

Figure 2.10   A graph illustration of all the IP addresses and devices used to review Restaurant 86 on September 9, 2014.

Each review is shown as a colored node, scaled from red to green, indicating the review rating. Associated with each review are three pieces of information:

- The business reviewed (building icon)
- The IP address used (computer icon)
- The device used to submit the review, whether it's a desktop or a mobile device (@ symbol icon)

Reviews flagged by the system as suspicious use a heavy red link instead of the default blue. Reviews previously removed as fraudulent show as ghosted red X nodes, as you can see in the detail in figure 2.11.

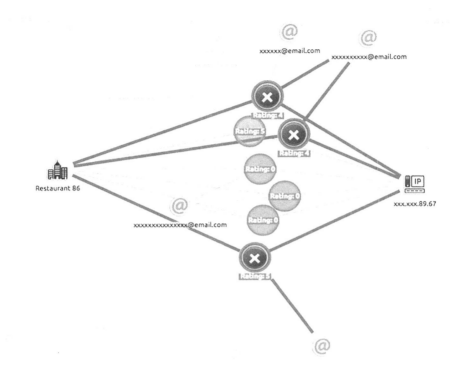

Figure 2.11   A closer look at a single review of Restaurant 86. This graph shows the email address, IP address, and five-star rating of Restaurant 86 by a single user, taken from figure 2.11.

In the center of the chart you can see an interesting cluster: One IP address has been used to submit seven reviews about a single business, using four different devices. Three reviews have already been removed as fake.

The timing and shared IP address of the remaining four mean they are also likely to be false. If we expand outward on one of the deleted reviews, we see more clues of a possible attempt to manipulate ratings, as shown in figure 2.12.

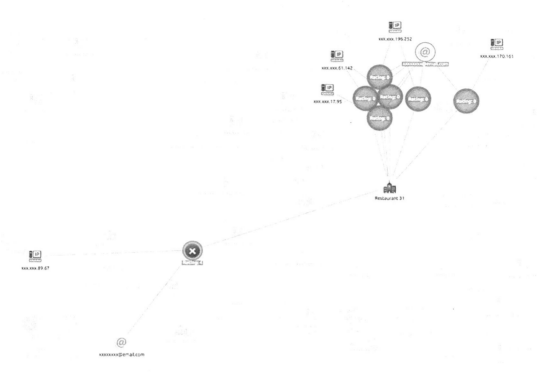

Figure 2.12   More suspicious patterns in the reviews of Restaurant 31. A user submitted eight reviews of Restaurant 31 under a single account, using five different IP addresses in an attempt to escape detection.

This time, one device has been used to submit eight zero-star reviews about a single business but using five different IP addresses (or, more likely, proxy IP addresses), probably to evade the reviewing software's protections that would flag the submissions as fraudulent.

There are many different ways to model review data, depending on the insight you need to uncover. In figure 2.13 we see three elements of the data:

- The reviewer's account (person nodes)
- The businesses being reviewed (building nodes)
- The review rating (green → red links)

Again, patterns instantly begin to stand out—not least the incredibly positive reviewer in the bottom left who has left dozens of five-star reviews for many different establishments.

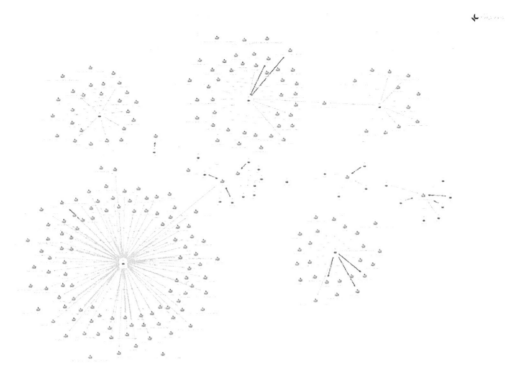

Figure 2.13   Patterns emerge in a graph visualization of restaurant reviews. Certain trends in the data pop when graphed, such as the possible astroturfing campaign by the reviewer in the bottom left, who leaves only positive reviews.

Could they be astroturfing, by using a fake account to write positive reviews for pay? Looking at the timing of the reviews, and the locations of the businesses being reviewed, would give some good insight.

Also of interest is a cluster in the middle, shown in figure 2.14.

We need to question why one business has received multiple one-star reviews from accounts that do not seem to have any other activity, a behavior we've identified as potential fraud.

Graph visualization has a significant role to play in detecting and investigating review fraud. Similar to credit card fraud, it's important to see what suspicious reviewers have in common with one another, such as sharing the same IP address or device. Representing the data as a graph and examining it visually can make a huge difference in the fight to ensure site content integrity.

Fraudulent reviews tend to stick out like a sore thumb in a graph visualization. Online review websites can use this technique to detect and delete fraudulent opinions,

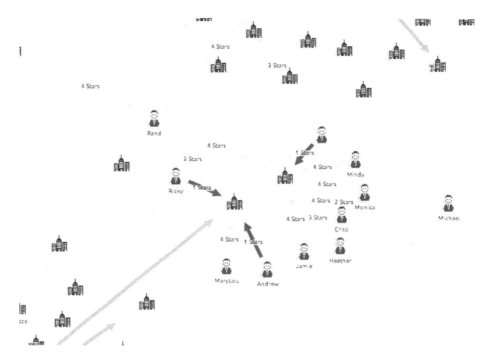

Figure 2.14 A closer look at a graph visualization of restaurant reviews. One restaurant has received multiple negative reviews from accounts with no other activity. What does this suggest?

whether it's a coordinated campaign of negative reviews posted against competitors or paid content posing as positive reviews.

2.3 *Cyber security*

Cyber security is a central concern for all organizations, but there's more than one way for a company or agency to protect its computer network from attack. As a result of the variety of ways to build and maintain an IT network, each organization has its own unique vulnerabilities.

Criminals, terrorists, and nation states, as well as activists and opportunistic amateurs, pose a real and persistent threat to corporate and government IT systems—a situation exacerbated by the complexity and variety of such systems. Cyber security professionals face an almost impossible task on three fronts:

- To proactively maintain a secure network perimeter
- To constantly monitor for new and emerging threats
- To detect, understand, and rectify previous attacks

Although many of us take the proper operation of computer networks for granted, there's a vast infrastructure of networking equipment and connections behind even the simplest network. As an increasing share of our lives take place on the internet—the largest network of all—how do we protect ourselves from malicious attacks?

Cyber security is a data-led battle, with terabytes of disparate information collated from around the enterprise into centralized dashboards, sometimes in dedicated network operations centers (NOCs) or security operations centers (SOCs).

Existing security information and event management (SIEM) tools do an excellent job of collating this data, often with automated real-time alerts. Unfortunately, most lack the visualization capabilities required to interpret the data as a big picture. This means alerts are not effectively investigated, and post-attack forensics are inefficiently managed. Graph visualization can be an effective approach to the manual investigation of real-time alerts and post-attack forensics, but performance implications must be considered. A graph visualization that tries to individually plot each IP packet as it flows across a network would be useless because the screen would be completely black from the number of nodes and links.

This section will guide you on using graphing tactics to enhance cyber security at your organization by helping to predict when an attack is imminent and then prevent it.

2.3.1 *Understanding unusual network traffic*

Understanding which outside networks traffic is going to is a key task in ensuring a secure network perimeter. Once an attacker has compromised the network, often the next step is to "call home" in order to accept the tasks requested by the hacker, for example, sending spam or collecting personal details or simply exporting data stolen from the network.

Similarly, high levels of inbound traffic should raise concerns, often indicating a large number of connection attempts and an imminent compromise.

The example in figure 2.15 shows a filtered view of IP connections on one corporate network. The traffic volume is indicated by the weight of the link (the wider the arrow, the heavier the volume) and the node color denotes its location—green is part of the network, red is external.

Nodes are clustered using a structural layout, so nodes with similar characteristics are grouped together. Such similarities might be IP connections within a single department, for example.

In figure 2.15, you can clearly see one external node (at roughly 10 o'clock) sending a high volume of traffic—potentially spammer requests—into the corporate network. Certain nodes are also sending high volumes externally. There could be rational explanations for both scenarios, or they could indicate an automated attack or internal compromise.

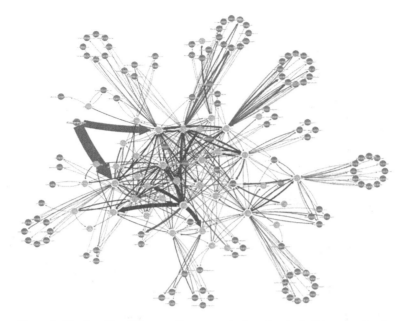

Figure 2.15 Graphing IP connections on a single network. In this example of a corporate network, traffic volume is represented by the edge (the wider the arrow, the heavier the volume) and the node color denotes whether an IP address is part of the network (green) or external (red).

2.3.2 *Deconstructing a botnet attack*

Botnets are a common cause of unusual traffic patterns, and they indicate that machines in your network may be participating in distributed denial of service (DDoS) attacks or spam campaigns. Botnets disrupt IT networks by causing computers to process large packets of malicious data.

Understanding the scale of the problem and finding all of the infected machines in a huge network can be challenging. Equally, understanding whether they are related or working together is virtually impossible without effective data visualization.

This first screenshot, figure 2.16, shows an unfiltered cut of traffic data taken from a university IT network and published by the Center for Applied Internet Data Analysis (http://bit.ly/1gk7Kl1). Nodes are IP addresses; the links are packets of data. Nodes are sized by the number of packets they're processing (inbound or out) and links are weighted by packet size. Links are also colored by protocol type. The unfiltered view, like the one shown here, is difficult to interpret.

In the next view, figure 2.17, we see the same data but filtered by node degree—that is, highlighting nodes with the most connections to other nodes. This quickly helps us find the most active machines in the network, filtering out the noise that we don't currently need to see. This is a quick and intuitive way to find machines in a network that have potentially been taken over by a botnet system.

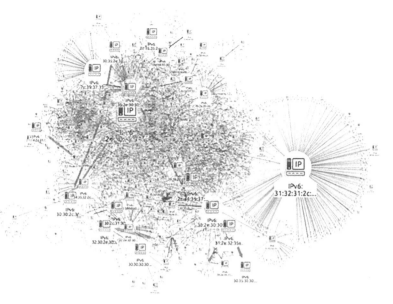

Figure 2.16   Unfiltered graph visualization of a university IT network under botnet attack. Nodes are IP addresses; the links are packets of data. Larger nodes denote the higher number of packets they're processing, both inbound and out. Links are weighted by packet size and colored by protocol type. Without filters, this representation is difficult to analyze.

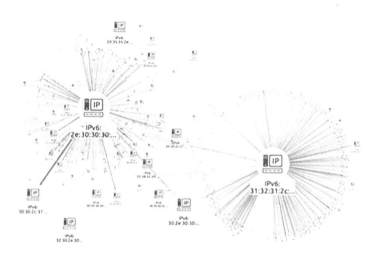

Figure 2.17   Filtered graph visualization of a university IT network under botnet attack. By applying a filter to highlight the nodes with the most connections to other nodes, we can quickly find the most active machines in the network. This is a quick and intuitive way to locate the machines in a network that have potentially been taken over by a botnet system.

2.3.3 *Analyzing malware propagation*

The fourth and, perhaps, most versatile cyber security use case for network visualization is to understand the propagation of malware, software maliciously designed to cause problems on the computer. This model can be used for multiple activities, such as the following:

- Understanding how far a known virus has spread and identifying compromised machines
- Modeling the threat posed by malware
- Tracking offensive hacking activity
- Monitoring honeypot traps

The next two charts show the propagation of malware through a deliberately infected corporate computer network. Twelve machines in the network were infected to see how the traffic spread to other machines. Over 7800 machines were included in the data set.

The first example, figure 2.18, shows the entire network in a single chart. Yellow links indicate benign traffic; red links indicate traffic with at least one infected packet. Already certain machines stand out as highly active.

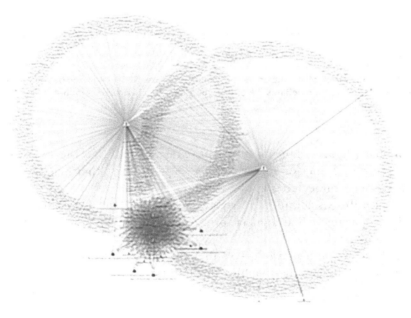

Figure 2.18 Identifying machines infected with malware. Yellow links indicate benign traffic in a corporate IT network; red links indicate traffic with at least one infected packet. Already certain machines stand out as highly active.

The next chart, figure 2.19, shows all the traffic coming from a single machine. Nodes are sized by volume of traffic, clearly showing which seven machines are disproportionately affected.

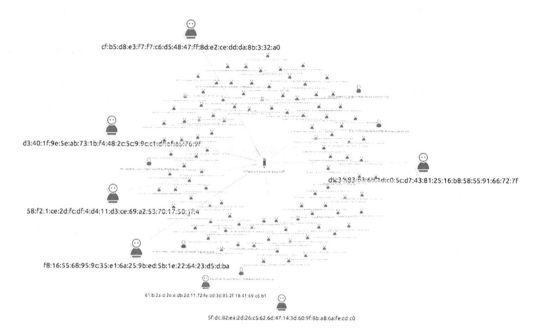

Figure 2.19   Identifying which machines have the most malware. Nodes are sized by volume of traffic, clearly showing which seven machines were disproportionately affected in a malware attack on a corporate IT network.

This final chart, figure 2.20, shows just the infected traffic in the network. We can identify the two machines originally infected, with the ten other machines forming a cluster in a tightly connected group in the top left.

Armed with this visualization, a cyber security professional can identify machines that would propagate malware quickly or can better understand the structure of a foreign infected network.

Unusual activity on a network—whether through DDoS attacks, botnets, or malware—can be graphed easily, enabling IT administrators to limit the damage caused by malicious attacks on their networks and improve their security going forward.

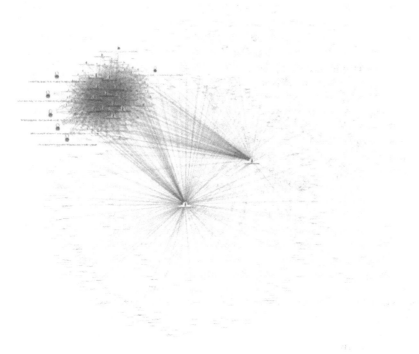

Figure 2.20 Isolating infected traffic in a malware attack. This graph helps identify the original two machines that were infected in a malware attack, with the ten other machines forming a cluster in a tightly connected group in the top left.

2.4 *Sales and marketing graphs*

The *social graph* is a hot new buzzword that appeals to brand marketers. They want to use the broad array of social networking data available across tools like Facebook and Twitter to better understand their brand's place in the mindset of their potential consumers and use that data to try to improve their brand reputation. Looking at a graph of this data can show some interesting results—not just who likes your company and what they're saying about it, but what other brands those same people like. In addition, graphs can be helpful in identifying *tastemakers*, people whose opinions are trusted and who have influence over a wide array of others. Those people can be given special treatment to ensure they have a good experience with your brand, and hopefully they'll broadcast that goodwill to their large following.

To illustrate this, I'll show an example from online poker. A couple of years ago, I worked with an entrepreneur who was interested in starting a magazine aimed at players of online poker and wanted to use social network analysis and graph visualization to understand who the most influential people were in the online poker world. We created a graph of the most active people or companies talking about poker on Twitter and who they follow. Initially, the graph looked like the one in figure 2.21.

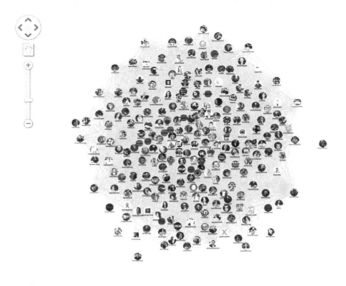

Figure 2.21   A graph of the most prominent Twitter users talking about poker

We modeled each tweeter as a node, with their Twitter avatar as their node icon. This messy graph didn't seem to get us any closer to answering the publisher's question: who do I have to win over, such that if I can get them to endorse my magazine, others will follow? In this graph, we learned that poker players are a tightly knit group, with most users following most other users, so there weren't obvious candidates for key influencers, but a couple of modifications to the graph helped us make some progress.

The first step was to reduce the amount we were trying to cram in the visualization all at once. Node-link visualizations aren't particularly helpful when everything is linked to everything else. To reduce the clutter, we needed some sort of criteria by which to filter the graph, to set a threshold for whether a link should be visible or not. Because we were looking for those influencers in the network, people who have a lot of reach, we used a social network analysis centrality score called *eigenvector centrality* to hide the less influential nodes and focus on the more central nodes. I mentioned betweenness earlier in the chapter—eigenvector centrality is another measure of node centrality, but this time we're focused on influence within the network. Without going into detail on the math, eigenvector centrality looks at how well connected each node is in a recursive process that looks not just at how many links each node has but whom those links are to and if they have high centrality scores as well.

In this poker chart, we applied a filter to remove the nodes with lower betweenness, because they aren't likely to be influencers in the poker world, and leave only the high-scoring ones. The result is shown in figure 2.22.

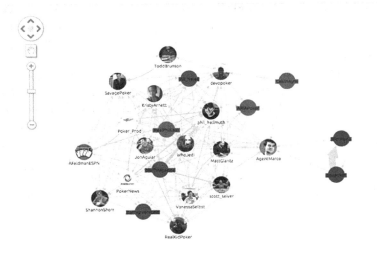

Figure 2.22   Nodes were filtered to show only those with high eigenvector scores, meaning the most influential in the network.

It's still a bit cluttered, but we're making progress. We're looking at only the most influential nodes from the previous graph. In the previous step, we filtered the nodes, but it can make sense to do so for the links as well. It's less important to see two nodes linked if they merely follow one another; perhaps we can focus only on those relationships that are stronger, where the two accounts have mentioned one another in tweets often. That result is depicted in figure 2.23.

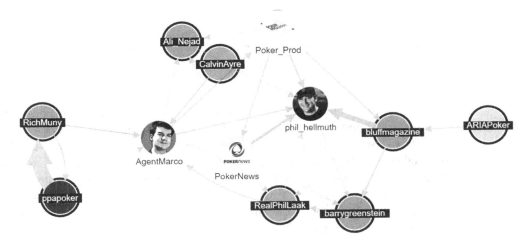

Figure 2.23   Links are filtered based on the relationship strength to show only those close connections.

This graph makes it clear that AgentMarco and phil_hellmuth are the two poker players with the most influence across the social poker network. The other nodes remaining on the chart are other media outlets and news aggregators. We also know their closest relationships on Twitter, so if we wanted to get to Marco or Phil, we could do that by first approaching one of their connections. But out of Marco and Phil, who is a better target for our new magazine? Who is likely to influence the run-of-the-mill poker player who will form our subscriber base? In the graph, we sized the nodes by the number of mentions, meaning the number of times that account is mentioned in the tweets of another. We can imagine that Twitter users who get mentioned often have a more active following than those who just have a lot of followers. People who have a lot of followers but few mentions may be famous but not engage much on Twitter.

By doing this, we got the chart shown in figure 2.24, which depicts Marco quite a bit larger than Phil.

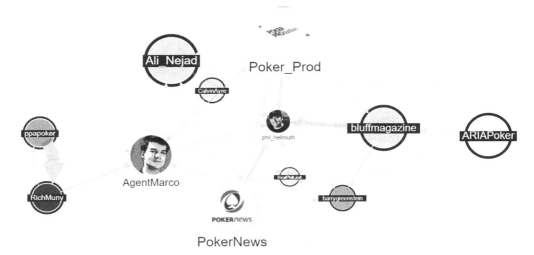

Figure 2.24   The nodes are sized by the number of mentions they get on Twitter.

This graph and visualization provide some insight into the social network surrounding poker players and their engagement with the poker community. By using some of the social network analysis centrality scores and some filtering on the graph, we were able to drill down into a large, seemingly intractable data set to determine who the most influential poker players are on Twitter, who their close connections are, and who are getting mentioned most often by their peers. Although a lot more would go into the decision than just social networking, my suggestion from the data would be to approach AgentMarco about a possible endorsement. I'll show you how to build your own graph from social network data in Gephi in chapter 3.

2.5 *Summary*

We've discussed a number of examples of graph visualizations used in different industries on real data and the value they can provide to a wide variety of users ranging from intelligence analysts to social marketing experts to security professionals.

- With large numbers of data endpoints, a zoomed-out view helps identify broader patterns in the data.
- Zooming in on the graph can reveal which nodes are acting as hubs, holding the graph together, and those nodes are often important, as was obvious in the terrorism graph.
- Filtering, or allowing the user to hide and show groups of nodes, helps to focus the graph on which pieces are relevant to the task at hand.
- Using visual properties of nodes and links such as size, color, and line thickness to map to properties in the data gives the user more information.
- Transactional networks rarely have large interconnected patterns; they're more likely to have starburst patterns. Large clusters can be indicative of fraudulent behavior.
- The social graph, or a network of social networking connections, can help marketers better understand consumer engagement with their brand.

In the next part of the book, we'll look at how to create graph visualization applications on your own data using a couple of available tools.

An introduction
to Gephi and KeyLines

This chapter covers

- A comparison of two graph visualization tools
- A short tutorial on Gephi
- Building visualization web applications with KeyLines
- A short tutorial on KeyLines

You have many different tools available to build graph visualizations, and selecting the right one depends on a number of different factors. Because the tools vary significantly in both their capabilities and their user interface, I selected two that I use in the examples in the rest of the book, Gephi and KeyLines. In the appendix, I discuss their capabilities and show a number of different examples using another graph visualization tool, D3. D3.js is a popular visualization library, but it's not the focus of this book for two reasons: First, it's a general-purpose visualization tool that covers many different types of visualizations, and graphs are only a small subset. In addition, D3 is a low-level library, which means that some of the concepts discussed in the later chapters of this book would require pages and pages of source code. For a more in-depth discussion of D3, see the book *D3.js in Action* by Elijah Meeks (Manning, 2015).

There are other graph visualization tools that I don't discuss in detail in this book, because the idiosyncrasies of each tool would be interesting only for those people using that tool and would drastically increase the length of the book. Many of the concepts that I discuss, although I use Gephi and KeyLines to visualize them, are applicable regardless of which application or library you use to create the visualizations. Table 3.1 lists of some of the more popular graph visualization libraries, and I'm certain there are others.

Table 3.1   A list of the more popular graph visualization tools

D3.js	http://www.d3js.org	Open source; does graph visualization among other visualizations; SVG rendering.
Cytoscape.js	http://www.cytoscape.org	Open source; mostly used for scientific data, but getting traction in other domains.
Cytoscape Web	http://www.cytoscape.org	Open source desktop application; recently deprecated in favor of Cytoscape.js but still useful.
GraphViz	http://www.graphviz.org	Open source; quite dated but a classic. Everybody has used it at some point.
Gephi	http://www.gephi.org	Desktop software for creating graph visualizations; lots of community plugins; used in this book.
KeyLines	http://www.keylines.com	Commercial software for building custom applications for graph visualization. Used in this book.

It matters significantly whether the goal is to visualize your own data or to build a graph visualization application where the end users want to explore their data but may not necessarily be data scientists. I chose Gephi because it's a well-known visualization tool that has been around for a number of years, it's relatively easy to use, and importing data sets from flat files is easy. It's free and open source, distributed under the GNU license, and can be downloaded here: http://www.gephi.org. I use the executable version of Gephi in these examples, but don't worry about the source. You're welcome to download and compile the Gephi source if you'd like. The result should be the same. At this time, Gephi 0.9.1 is the most current version; if you have a later version, the results in the tutorial may not be identical but should be similar.

Gephi is a great application, and because it's community supported, it has plugins to work with a number of different sources such as graph databases; but it's limited by the fact that it's a desktop (Windows, Mac, or Linux) application. It's designed for a single user, and its UI assumes quite a bit of technical knowledge to use properly. When rolling out a business application, it may be desirable to have a web-based graph application that has only the features and design that you choose. This is why I chose KeyLines as the other example toolkit. It's not an end-user-facing application itself but rather a JavaScript library for building web applications with a graph visualization component. As such, it's more customizable, but it does require JavaScript programming to attach to your data and to create the appearance and functionality you desire.

It's also neither open source nor free, but evaluation versions are available. You can request one at http://www.keylines.com. Full disclosure: I work for Cambridge Intelligence, the company that makes KeyLines.

3.1   *Gephi*

Gephi is an open source application created by the Gephi Consortium, a French non-profit company with members around the globe who help shape the requirements and drive the future development of the product. It's an extensible desktop application, and many plugins are available from the community. We'll use the basic Gephi application without any customization in this tutorial, but I'll demonstrate advanced features in later chapters.

In this tutorial, we'll use Gephi to analyze the social media response surrounding Boston's bid for the 2024 Olympic Games. As I write this, there's intense controversy surrounding the Olympic bid, with about half of Massachusetts supporting the bid and half opposed. We'll create a network of people discussing the matter on Twitter and see what we can learn. This will progress in three stages: first, we'll obtain some data using Netlytic; then, we'll import that into Gephi; and third, we'll customize the visualization using some of the features in Gephi. Because inevitably the data you see on Twitter will be different from what I got running this analysis in late 2015, I've made my data available on the Manning site for this book.

3.1.1   *Acquiring data*

To get your Twitter data, you'll use a tool called Netlytic, hosted at http://www.netlytic .org. The free version of their product allows you to maintain up to 1000 records in three different data sets, which is enough for our purposes.

Once you've created a free account and linked it to your Twitter handle, you'll see a tab called New Dataset. Here, you'll tell Netlytic to find all Twitter posts related to a specific username or hashtag. We'll use *boston2024* as our search term and get the last 1000 Twitter posts to use this hashtag. The next web page shows a table of the collected tweets and looks something like figure 3.1.

Right now, this is just a list of tweets and not a network. A network requires connections between the data elements, which in this case is the Twitter accounts and the references to other Twitter accounts in those tweets. To do that, we'll skip the tab labeled Text Analysis, as shown in figure 3.2, and proceed directly to the fourth tab, Network Analysis, shown in figure 3.3.

This process will automatically scour each tweet in your data set looking for both the poster and all the referenced accounts. Each account will be represented by a node, and each tweet that mentions other accounts will be represented as a link between the poster and those other accounts. So the first tweet in my data set, as shown previously in figure 3.1, is a tweet from 02129toonie that tags the @NoBosOlympics account. This will be represented in the network as a link from the 02129toonie node to the NoBosOlympics node. If there are multiple tweets from 02129toonie that mention NoBosOlympics, this

LINK	PUBDATE	AUTHOR	TITLE
http://twitter.com/02129toonie/statuses/611994281440604160	2015-06-19	02129toonie	RT @NoBosOlympics: The biggest costs of an Olympics arent venue construction, theyre the opportunity costs of more important things pushe…
http://twitter.com/103IBEW/statuses/612047621172166656	2015-06-19	103IBEW	Dorchester Avenue would be Olympic thoroughfare http://t.co/zClh600BKg @BostonGlobe #Boston2024 #Olympics
http://twitter.com/413Tweets/statuses/612246963111755776	2015-06-20	413Tweets	RT @efalchuk: Except the senate voted 22-17 against a measure that would have barred their use for #Boston2024. https://t.co/3UGHpryERc
http://twitter.com/4Coppinger/statuses/611992230174289920	2015-06-19	4Coppinger	RT @BrendanMJoyce: We are anxious to open our doors & share our nation & hospitality with participants & spectators from all over the worl…
http://twitter.com/4Coppinger/statuses/611995798151299072	2015-06-19	4Coppinger	MUST READ: Some opposing #Boston2024 need be civil especially to reporters covering this story. @jayfallon @leung http://t.co/z1CDIMLPrF

Figure 3.1   A table of tweets about the Boston 2024 Olympics bid. Reading each tweet would be tedious and you'd miss connections among them.

1. Edit   2. Preview   3. Text Analysis   4. Network Analysis   5. Report

Figure 3.2   The five steps to obtaining Twitter data with Netlytic

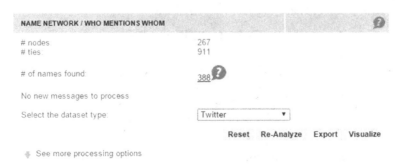

Figure 3.3   The Network Analysis page in Netlytic

will show up in a weight property on the link. You can see a list of the nodes collected by clicking the link next to # of Names Found. Now you need to export this data into a file format that Gephi understands. Click the Export button. (Don't click the Visualize button—this would bring up a sigma.js implementation that isn't very functional. I discuss sigma in the appendix.) Netlytic will give you the option to export in either UCI-Net format or Pajek format, and Gephi accepts both. We'll use Pajek in this example; the difference is just in the formatting of the text file and not substantial. After you click Export and choose the format, Netlytic will email you a link to download the file.

3.1.2 *Importing data into Gephi*

Gephi natively understands the Pajek format of the file you saved from Netlytic, so upon opening Gephi and creating a new project, it's a straightforward process to import that data into Gephi. You shouldn't receive any errors, but the initial result looks terrible. Figure 3.4 shows the initial view in Gephi of a thousand tweets about the Boston 2024 Olympic bid.

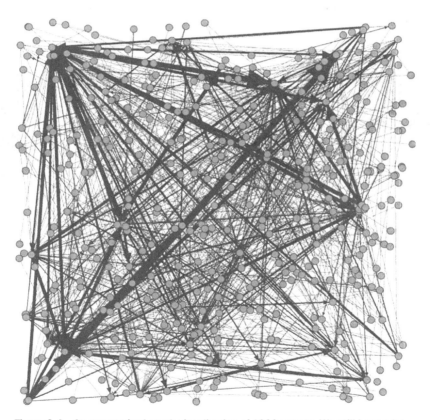

Figure 3.4   An unorganized graph visualization of 1000 tweets. We still have a lot of work to do to make this useful.

You'll learn more from the original table than from this visualization. But some of the power of Gephi lies in the tools that allow you to parse through this data, laying out the nodes, filtering, and coloring the nodes and links to help make sense of it.

3.1.3 *Visually organizing the data with layouts*

A number of different layout algorithms are built into Gephi, and they appear on the Layouts pane on the left side of the window. If you can't find it, the pane may be hidden; click Layout from the Window menu to restore it. From there, you can change the location of the nodes from the random placement where Gephi loads the data to an organization that makes more sense and is easier to read. We'll go into more detail on layouts in part 2 of this book, but for now, I encourage you to play around with the layout options and see which ones produce useful results. In my data set, the Fruchterman-Reingold layout makes for the most readable chart—it's a variation on the standard force-directed layouts that model the chart using principles from physics. The result is shown in figure 3.5. It's a more pleasant diagram but still not particularly useful.

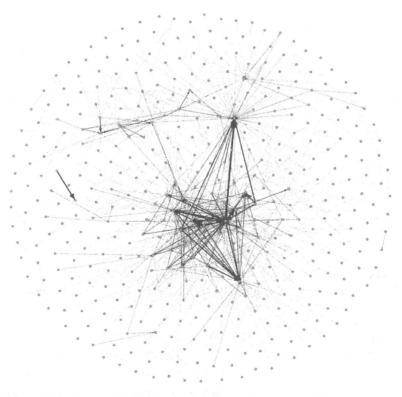

Figure 3.5 After the Fruchterman-Reingold layout has been applied, you start to see the central pattern. Remember that wide edges mean multiple tweets.

Force-directed layouts

The *force-directed* series of layouts model the chart as a spring, creating an attractive force for two nodes that have a link between them, as well as a repulsion force for two nodes that aren't connected. It then calculates the vector for the force on each node and moves that node the appropriate distance in the calculated direction. This process is repeated until each node is no longer moving (or until a predetermined number of iterations has been run). The scale of the forces can often be customized, allowing the user to determine the compactness of the chart: a high attractive force compared to the repulsive force will result in small, tight charts, and the opposite force will result in charts that are widely spread apart. The value of a layout like this is that it tends to put the best-connected nodes near the center of the chart, and isolated nodes with few connections end up far from the middle. I discuss layouts in more detail in chapter 7.

You can see a key group in the center of the network who are tweeting each other a lot and then some isolated nodes on the edges that have only one or two connections, but there's no indication of which accounts those are. For that you need labels.

3.1.4   Know what you're looking at with labels

Labels are important in a graph visualization. You have to be able to tell what you're looking at; otherwise, it's just a pretty picture. But labels can also get in the way. If there's too much text on either the nodes or the links, it can obscure the network structure and make it difficult to discern patterns. The gray *T* icon at the bottom left of the graph view allows you to turn labels off and on, and the sliders to the right of that icon allow you to control the size, color, and opacity of the label text. Be careful about adding too many labels to the chart because the layout algorithms don't take the label size into account when deciding on positions for nodes. Therefore, labels can overlap one another, making it very difficult to read. The image in figure 3.6 shows the chart with labels for each node. It's still a mess because we're trying to plot too much data at once.

3.1.5   Filtering

The next step we'll take with this data is to filter it. Filtering is the most basic way of paring down the size of a visualization to show only the nodes and edges that are relevant to the analysis. Gephi has a robust filtering engine that allows you to define complex filter queries that control visibility. In this case, we care less about those isolated nodes that have only one or two connections to the rest of the network; those accounts may have been mentioned in one or two tweets but are unlikely to be central to our understanding. Let's remove them and make the chart less cluttered.

We'll filter based on *node degree*, which is a score on each node counting the number of links it has. Here we'll just look at Degree, which doesn't care whether those

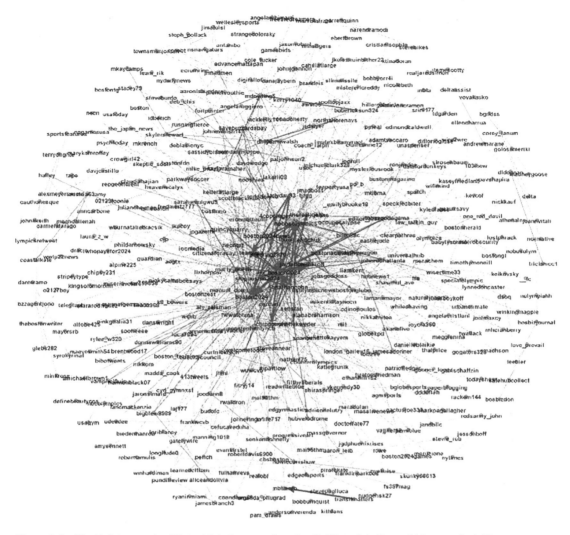

Figure 3.6 The Twitter graph with text labels on each node. At this point, they add too much clutter.

links point toward or away from the node. But if direction were important, we could instead use In Degree or Out Degree, which counts just that. We want to hide nodes that have fewer than 6 links, so on the right-hand Filter panel, expand the Topology folder and drag the Degree Range item down to the lower pane where it says Queries. After you do that, a slider bar appears at the bottom, allowing you to determine the range of degree scores that should be shown. Here we'll select 6 to 100, meaning any node with more than 6 and fewer than 100 links should be shown, but if it has fewer than 6 links, hide it. The result is shown in figure 3.7; it creates a more readable chart, though you may want to rerun the layout.

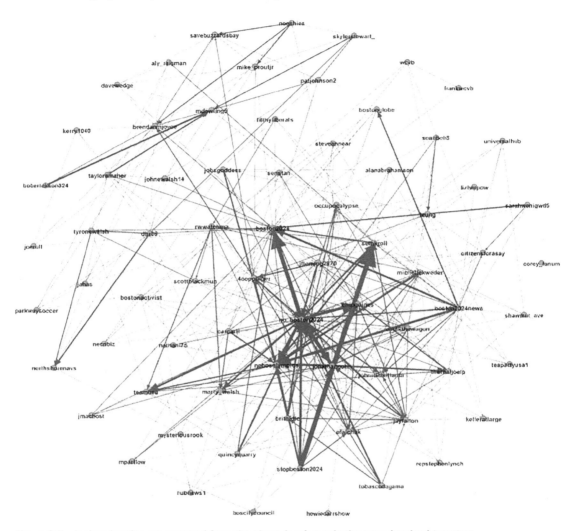

Figure 3.7   Isolated nodes are removed from the chart, leaving only the more involved tweeters.

You can identify some of the key accounts in this network: no_boston2024, a key account probably opposing the Olympic bid (based on the name); marty_walsh, the official account of the current Boston mayor; and bostonglobe, the Twitter account for the major local newspaper. We're still not learning as much from this chart as we could, so next we'll try adding size and color.

3.1.6   *Size*

The human brain and eye implicitly assume that larger items are more important than smaller items. Therefore, size is a valuable metric to use on both nodes and links to indicate importance, however you want to define that. In this case, we want to draw the user's eye to the key accounts that are holding this chart together. To do this, we'll take advantage of another centrality score that Gephi uses called *eigenvector centrality*. It's a recursive algorithm that gives high scores to nodes that have lots of links to other nodes that are themselves highly linked. To calculate eigenvector centrality, we'll select the Statistics pane, which is a separate tab next to the Filters tab in Gephi, and run the eigenvector centrality algorithm under Node Overview. This won't change the visualization, but it does make those scores available to bind to visual properties of the nodes on the chart.

To do that, we'll move over to the Appearance pane to the left of the graph visualization. *Appearance* is Gephi's term for scaling some visual property of the nodes or links on the chart to a property in the data. We'll start with size, so with the Nodes pane selected, click the icon with the three different-size circles to the right of the palette. Then select the Attributes tab, and in the drop-down where it says Choose An Attribute, select Eigenvector Centrality, the measure that you just calculated previously.

You can play with the metrics here to get a pleasing result—I had the best luck with a smallest size of 5 and a largest size of 80. By default, the size will vary linearly with the metric selected, which works well for centrality scores, but if you're sizing by a metric that varies widely, you may want to use the spline tool instead. This applies a custom nonlinear transformation of your own, or you can use one of the templates provided, such as logarithmic. The linear template works for this example. You can set this by clicking Spline. Figure 3.8 shows the result. Some of the key accounts in this Twitter debate are now becoming apparent.

3.1.7   *Color*

Now we'll partition the nodes into groups. This is called *community detection*, and Gephi does this by assigning nodes into categories based on their common links. Back on the Statistics pane, click Run (next to Modularity). We'll stick with the default parameters for now, but you can fine-tune these if Gephi is identifying too many or two few communities.

> **DEFINITION**   *Community* is a precise term when discussing graphs. This is a group of nodes with more links between members of the community than from members to other nodes. For example, in the social network of my friends on Facebook, there are easily identifiable groups of friends. My college classmates all know one another, my coworkers all know one another, and my neighbors all know one another, but there are few links among those groups other than through me. As a result, they form communities.

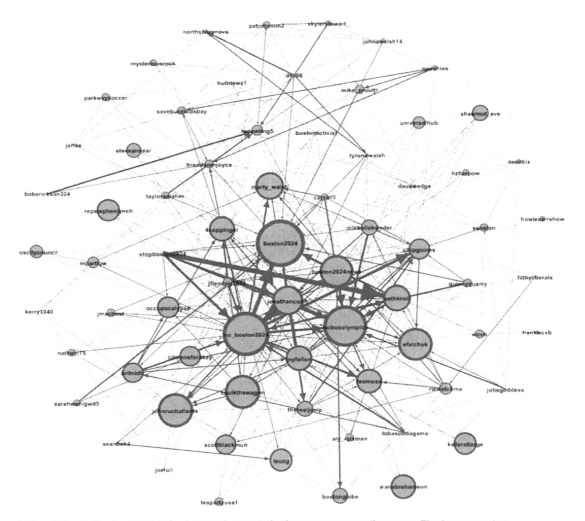

Figure 3.8   Nodes have been sized according to their eigenvector centrality score. The largest nodes have the widest influence throughout the network.

In my data set, Gephi identified five discrete communities of nodes of varying sizes. Now we want to color the nodes based on this community over on the Partition pane, next to Ranking on the left. On the Nodes tab, the drop-down will list all the metrics that have discrete values. Right now, Modularity Class is the only one. Selecting this will assign a color to each node based on the community in which it was found. The result of running the Fruchterman-Reingold layout again to clean things up is shown in figure 3.9. Although the figure is shown in grayscale in the printed book, the colored insert of this book has a reproduction in full color.

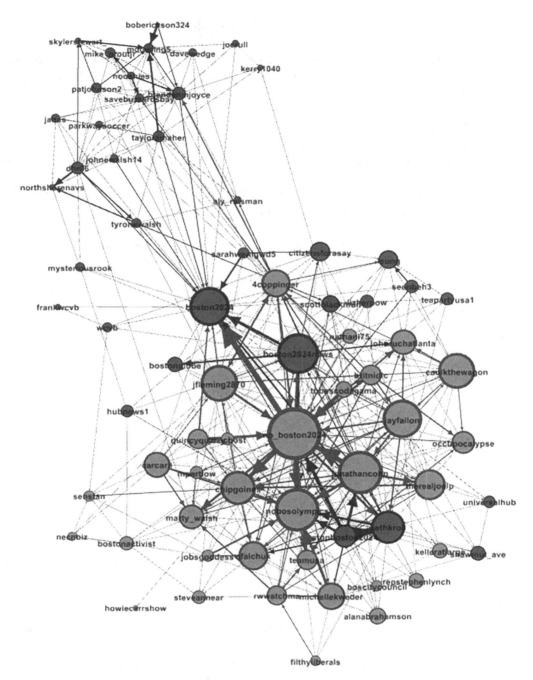

Figure 3.9 The graph of tweets after nodes have been colored by community. The colors now tell us who belongs to which group: pro-Olympics, anti-Olympics, or neutral.

Community detection isn't magic; it's just identifying these groups based on who tweets to whom. But those patterns can be revealing. Groups with lots of internal links and few external ones are likely to have something in common, and among those tweeting about the Boston Olympics bid, the groups would naturally be supportive of or opposed to the bid.

3.1.8   *Final product*

The result, after layouts, sizing, filtering, and coloring, is a usable graph visualization showing the communities on Twitter surrounding the Boston 2024 bid. In this visualization, Gephi has colored green those accounts opposed to the bid (like no_boston2024 and nobosolympics) and the connections among them. The key accounts are sized larger so they catch the eye. You can see that this is a tight-knit group, with most members of the group mentioning at least once most other members of the group. (Gephi isn't perfect; Marty Walsh, the mayor in favor of the bid, was colored green by the algorithm because he is mentioned far more often by Twitter users opposed to the bid than those in favor.) The purple color was assigned to the official accounts or neutral parties like boston2024, the official Twitter account for the bid; boston2024news; or bostonglobe, the Twitter account for the newspaper. The red color is assigned to those in favor of the bid. As you can see, there are very few links from one group to another. In fact, other than the official accounts, the user 4coppinger is the only one directly engaging with both sides. Thus, if I were a neutral arbitrator trying to identify someone who can resolve this dispute, that user would be a natural choice.

In summary, Gephi is a great tool for someone who's familiar with their data, understands both data modeling and graph algorithms, and wants a point-and-click interface to produce a static visualization. It can generate great results quickly, and because it's a desktop product instead of a web-based one, it can work with larger graphs. Graphs with 10,000 nodes are easy to work with. The drawbacks to Gephi are that it's a community-supported (meaning poorly documented) tool that's still in beta; it's desktop-based, so it can't support a large community of users; and it requires an understanding of graph theory—although the latest 0.9 release represents a significant step forward. KeyLines, which we'll look at next, is a web-based toolkit for integrating graph visualization into your own web application, which means that it's more customizable but requires JavaScript programming and has some performance limitations when it comes to large graphs.

3.2   *KeyLines*

Although Gephi is great for building your own visualizations, for a truly interactive experience, sometimes a better solution is to build a visualization application yourself or roll graph visualization capability into your existing web application. For that, KeyLines is a good fit. This section is a brief introduction to KeyLines, so I assume you have a basic understanding of JavaScript and web application development concepts. I don't go into detail about web server hosting, development environments, or database development. For a refresher, Neal Ford's *Art of Java Web Development* (Manning, 2003) is a good start.

KeyLines is a commercial JavaScript component that does the rendering of graph visualizations in a web browser and is designed to be a supported component inside enterprise environments. It has function calls to add and manipulate data on the chart, as well as events that capture user actions (such as click, double-click, and drag-and-drop) to allow you to capture that action and have the application respond. Although this allows for quite a bit of flexibility, it also creates some complexity, and there are some challenges to getting KeyLines to behave the way you'd expect. Here, we'll walk through a short tutorial on building a web application using KeyLines and adding some sample data. This is a basic example to get you started. We'll build on this in each chapter, adding more-complex capabilities as we go. By the end of the book, we'll have a powerful graph-visualization application.

> **Downloading KeyLines and configuring your JavaScript environment**
>
> Unlike Gephi, KeyLines is neither free nor open source, but Cambridge Intelligence, the company behind KeyLines, allows for free two-month evaluations of the tool. You can request those evaluations at http://cambridge-intelligence.com/visualizing-graph-data/.

You can use any JavaScript-compatible development application when working with KeyLines. Here, we'll just use a generic text editor to keep things simple. I prefer Text-Mate because I like the syntax highlighting, but anything will work. It's free for download at https://macromates.com/download.

3.2.1 Encode an HTML page

The next step is to create an HTML page that will contain KeyLines. The full HTML code is downloadable from this book's website, so there's no need to retype anything.

In your HTML page, you need to add the references to the KeyLines JavaScript files:

```
<script src="js/keylines.js"></script>
<script src="js/jquery-1.10.1.js"></script>
```

You also need to tell the page about the custom fonts being used by KeyLines. This just requires adding a reference to the CSS file in the /fonts folder:

```
<link rel="stylesheet" type="text/css" href="css/keylines.css">
```

This test page will have only KeyLines in it, which itself will be in a DIV element, so add the following line in the body section of the HTML:

```
<div class="box" id ="drawingID" style="width: 818px; height: 586px; border:
4px;"></div>
```

As you add more functionality to your KeyLines application, this section will become more complex.

3.2.2   *Write KeyLines JavaScript*

Now you have an HTML file. Next, you need to add additional JavaScript to load Key-Lines and give it some data to visualize. Although typically you'd add this as a separate JavaScript file, for this tutorial you'll embed it directly in the HTML file:

```
<script>
$(window).load(function () {

KeyLines.mode('canvas');                          Set the
                                                  rendering
KeyLines.setCanvasPaths('assets/');               mode
KeyLines.create ('drawingID', /*id*/                        Set a path to
                         callback); /*callback*/            the assets
});
function callback(err, chart) {                             Load the component:
 chart.load({                                               specify the id and
   type: 'LinkChart',                                       callback
   items: [{id:'id1', type: 'node', x:150, y: 150, t:'Hello World!'}]
 });
}
</script>
```

`create` will find the DIV element with the ID given (in this case, `drawingID`) and replace it with the KeyLines component. `chart.load` will load your chart with the data given to it as documented in the Object Formats page of the KeyLines Evaluation site.

Load the page in your browser, and you should have a working KeyLines application, albeit a very simple one, as shown in figure 3.10.

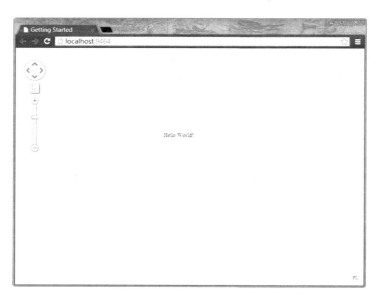

Figure 3.10   A KeyLines chart running inside Google Chrome. There's no data on this chart yet other than a single Hello World! node.

3.2.3 *Bind KeyLines to data*

The most common use of KeyLines is to visualize data from an existing data store, whether that's a graph database like Neo4j, Titan, or InfiniteGraph, or a relational database queried by SQL or some other method.

For the purpose of this tutorial, we'll do the following:

- Load a JSON string using the Ajax functions in jQuery
- Parse it using some JavaScript
- Load the KeyLines chart with the data already present

The following listing shows some simple sample data in JSON format. Copy it as a file named JSONFile.json to the root folder of your website.

Listing 3.1 The JSON object representing the nodes and links to show

```json
{
  "items": {
    "nodes": {
      "node": [
        {
          "id": "1",
          "name": "Charles",
          "color": "blue"
        },
        {
          "id": "2",
          "name": "Grace",
          "color": "black"
        },
        {
          "id": "3",
          "name": "Stephen",
          "color": "red"
        },
        {
          "id": "4",
          "name": "Carlos",
          "color": "green"
        }
      ]
    },
    "edges": {
      "edge": [
        {
          "id": "5",
          "endfrom": "1",
          "endto": "4",
          "strength": "4"
        },
        {
          "id": "6",
          "endfrom": "4",
          "endto": "3",
```

```
            "strength": "1"
        },
        {
          "id": "7",
          "endfrom": "2",
          "endto": "4",
          "strength": "10"
        },
        {
          "id": "8",
          "endfrom": "2",
          "endto": "3",
          "strength": "1"
        }
      ]
    }
  }
}
```

The structure of this file is quite simple. There are two lists:

- *Nodes*, each with a unique ID
- *Edges*, the relationships between those nodes, with `"endfrom"` and `"endto"` being the two endpoints

The nodes and edges have tags defining characteristics:

- *Name tag* defines the node label.
- *Color tag* defines the color of the node KeyLines draws.
- *Strength* defines the width of the links.

Next, use JQuery's Ajax function to load the JSON file into memory so it can be queried—it should replace the previous callback:

```
function callback(err, chart) {
    $.ajax({
        type: "GET",
        url: "JSONFile.json",
        dataType: "json",
        success: function (json) {
            ParseJSONData(json, chart);
        }
    })
}
```

Add this to your callback function under `window.load` in the previous function.

Now that you have the JSON object in memory, you need to create the KeyLines JSON from the source data. Add this function to your code:

```
function ParseJSONData(JSONObject, chart) {        Iterate through each
                                                   node in your JSON data
    var requestData = new Object();
    requestData.type = 'LinkChart';               Set up the properties
    requestData.items = [];                        of the chart object
```

```
                    for (var i = 0; i < JSONObject.items.nodes.node.length; i++) {
                        var nodeid = JSONObject.items.nodes.node[i].id;
                        var nodename = JSONObject.items.nodes.node[i].name;
                        var nodecolor = JSONObject.items.nodes.node[i].color;
                        requestData.items.push({ id: nodeid, type: 'node', t: nodename,
                    c: nodecolor })
                    }
                    for (var j = 0; j < JSONObject.items.edges.edge.length; j++) {
                        var edgeid = JSONObject.items.edges.edge[j].id;
                        var edgefrom = JSONObject.items.edges.edge[j].endfrom;
                        var edgeto = JSONObject.items.edges.edge[j].endto;
                        var strength = JSONObject.items.edges.edge[j].strength;
                        requestData.items.push({ id: edgeid, type: 'link', id1: edgefrom,
                    id2: edgeto, w: strength })
                    }
                    chart.load(requestData);
                    chart.layout();
                }
```

Create the JSON object for each node → (points to the node push line)

Get each node from the JSON file → (points to nodecolor line)

Run the standard layout → (points to chart.layout())

Load the chart with the data created in the earlier loop → (points to chart.load)

Create the JSON object for the link, using the width of the link as the strength → (points to edge push line)

Get the details of each edge → (points to strength line)

You should now have a working KeyLines application that's loading the external data (from memory) and displaying it as a graph, as shown in figure 3.11.

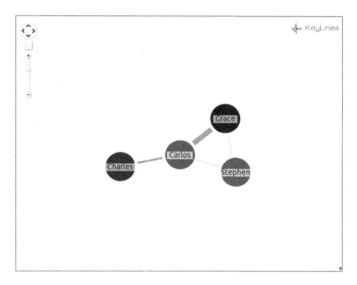

Figure 3.11 A simple KeyLines chart using the JSON data we specified

3.3 *Summary*

In this chapter, you gained a fundamental understanding of the strengths and weaknesses of both Gephi and KeyLines, learned when using one or the other may be most appropriate, given your requirements, and took a shallow dive into how to create graph visualizations using each of these tools.

Gephi:

- Is best for data scientists viewing their own data
- Visualizes data mainly from flat files, although database connectors do exist as plugins
- Is community developed and community supported
- Is open source and free

KeyLines:

- Is a JavaScript library for graph visualization in a web browser
- Interacts with data through JSON
- Can be embedded inside a larger web application
- Allows for interactivity by capturing user actions
- Is commercial software and closed source

Part 2

Visualize your own data

In part two of this book, we'll dive down into some of the techniques that will help you provide compelling, effective visualizations, using both Gephi and Key-Lines, and you'll learn how to avoid some of the pitfalls that can confuse your chart readers. First, we'll address styling: how to convey interesting, relevant information in your graphs and how to avoid unhelpful clutter. Second, we'll discuss interactivity: how to get your users involved in your visualizations so that they can find what they want and look at the data at the level that's appropriate for them. Then, we'll discuss a few detailed topics for specific types of graphs, for example, how to work with dynamic graphs—graphs that change over time—and geospatial graphs—where the data contains spatial coordinates. In the technical appendix, I provide some sample source code to get started visualizing graphs with D3.js, a popular data visualization library.

Data modeling

I hope that the first few chapters have convinced you of the value of graphs, but most data isn't conveniently organized into nodes and links. In this chapter, I'll show you how to take data in tabular or key-value format and represent it in terms of nodes and links so that it can be visualized. Data is rarely natively organized in a way that's useful in a graph, so it must be restructured.

Imagine your data as a number of large spreadsheets. In order to visualize this data as a graph, you'd have to pick through the entries in the spreadsheets to determine which entries represent nodes, which entries represent relationships, and which entries can be discarded. That process is called *data modeling*. A graph model is a logical view of the data elements and their connections to each other, disregarding how the data is stored in a database. A data model is a question you wish to answer with your data. There can be many different graph models of the same data. In this chapter, I'll show you how to derive a model from different sorts of data and talk about some of the tools such as graph databases that allow you to store the data efficiently in graph format to avoid the modeling task altogether.

4.1   What is a data model?

A data model defines the structure of a set of data, helping to determine what the real-life elements are in a data set, such as people, cars, and locations, and how they're related to each other. Every organized data set has a data model, even if it's not explicitly defined. In this section, we'll look at how to model both tabular data and key-value stores as a graph to make visualization easier and more intuitive.

4.1.1   Relational data

Relational databases have been around since the 1960s and are still the primary method of storing digital data, because they use a very intuitive format. Relational data is called tabular data because the data is represented in one or more tables with records (rows) representing real-world objects. Although it's most often visualized in a grid, there's a lot of value in visualizing this data as a graph, but it must be transformed, because tables of columns and rows aren't always easy to convert to nodes and links.

Imagine the following four-table relational database, shown in tables 4.1 through 4.4.

Table 4.1   A sample student registry

Key	First name	Last name	Telephone number
1	Corey	Lanum	775-6665
2	Stella	Gerrity	431-1411
3	Toby	Quenton	810-9184
4	Marie	Jeanne	481-2414

Table 4.2   A sample teacher registry

Key	First name	Last name	Extension
1	Ronan	Christianson	516-4125
2	Josie	Larkin	431-1411
3	Neige	LaFontaine	516-8637
4	Ferris	McGillicutty	410-7314

Table 4.3 A sample teacher directory

Key	Teacher	Name
1	4	Constitutional Law
2	1	Beach Safety
3	2	Calculus II
4	3	Conversational French

Table 4.4 A sample class registration, combining data elements from tables 4.1 and 4.3

Student	Class
1	4
1	3
2	3
2	4
2	1
3	1
4	2
4	1
4	4

In this simple example, the database describes students, teachers, classes, and which teachers and students participate in which classes. The data model defines that structure: each class has one teacher but can have an arbitrary number of students. The relationships here are implicit, but we can assume that a teacher's relationship to a class is that they teach it, and a student is registered for the class. The fourth table allows us to link multiple students with a single class. Table 4.4 is necessary in an RDBMS because each table must have a fixed number of columns, not allowing us to have a table that lists all students in each class.

To define a model is simply to make this structure explicit, represented as a graph in figure 4.1.

Many people will build the data model first and then fit their data into it. This helps organize the data in a way that allows it to be easily understood, at the expense of being less flexible if data arrives that doesn't fit the model. If that happens, you'll need to start over with a new data model. This has led to the explosion of *schemaless* databases, which allow their model to be extended on the fly.

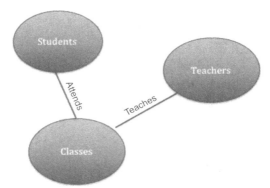

Figure 4.1   **A graph representing the relationships in the previous tables. This graph model closely resembles the table structure of the database. In this data model, we've chosen to represent students, teachers, and classes from the four tables as nodes.**

So a data model is a description of the real-world objects contained in the data. In the first model, it roughly aligns with our table structure (which would help if your question is about which students take classes with which professors) and treats the phone numbers as properties of the student and teacher nodes. But you could easily pick another question to answer where the phone information is front and center. If you were using this data to uncover calling patterns, you might prefer a different model, like the one in figure 4.2. This would help reveal that a student shares a phone number with a teacher.

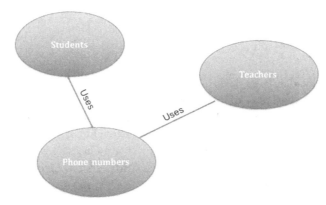

Figure 4.2   **This graph is an alternative model for the tabular data shown previously. There is no table for phone numbers, but it might make sense, if the question about the data involves phones, to model the phone numbers as a node.**

4.1.2   *Key-value stores*

The relationship between the physical model and the logical model can become even more tenuous when you have a large key-value store in a database such as CouchDB. Consider the data in the following listing, which is a list of keys and values. It's some of the same data as in the tables in the previous section, but I haven't listed the entire set.

Listing 4.1   A subset of the tabular database, represented as a series of key-values

```
{name: 'Corey Lanum', role:'student'}
{name: 'Corey Lanum', phoneNumber:'775-6665'}
{name: 'Corey Lanum', class: 'Conversational French'}
{name: 'Corey Lanum', class: 'Calculus II'}
{name: 'Ferris McGillicutty', role: 'professor'}
{name: 'Ferris McGillicutty', class: 'Constitutional Law'}
```

This is a subset of the data identified in tables 4.1–4.4, but there's no structure imposed on the data. Although you've seen students, teachers, and classes so far, the next record could involve pets with an entirely new set of properties. It's a bit tougher to impose a model on data stored like this, but it is possible, and both figures 4.1 and 4.2 are plausible models for this data. Key-value stores are used because of their flexibility. They are schemaless, which means that there's no need to categorize in advance what sort of data you'll add next. In order to impose a model on this data, you need to look at which values are being used most often and decide whether those represent properties of the objects or the objects themselves.

A data model is an organizational structure for data, and its design is dependent on the questions you want to answer with your data. In the next section, we'll look at the graph model, introduced in chapter 1, which organizes data in terms of nodes and links and allows it to be visualized with a node-link diagram.

4.2   Graph data models

Models are useful for a number of different reasons and help you better understand the data contained in the database. A graph model is just one type of data model, which itself is often represented as a graph. It's simply a list of the nodes and links derived from your data, how they're connected to each other, and where in the data those items can be found. Figures 4.1 and 4.2 are graph models of the tabular data from tables 4.1–4.4.

4.2.1   Identifying nodes

Because a graph model is a list of the node and link types in the data, the first step is to identify the nodes. This is easy when the node type is represented by a table in the database, such as students and teachers in our example, but it's a different situation when you want nodes to represent concrete things that aren't entire tables in your database, such as phones. There, you need to come up with how to define a unique item in your data. In the case of phones, the phone number uniquely identifies a phone (and it's the only property we have related to the phones), so even though we don't have a phone table, we can find each instance of each unique phone number in the data and merge those records to represent a single phone, as shown in figure 4.3.

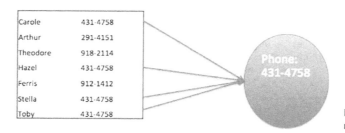

Figure 4.3   A duplicated phone number can indicate a single entity

The selection of which property to use as that unique identifier is important, especially if we're going to then visualize that data. Although we might be able to get away with merging each instance of "Corey Lanum" in the data into a single node representing me, someone named "David Smith" might object, because there could be dozens of people with the same name in the data who are actually separate people, as shown in the example in figure 4.4.

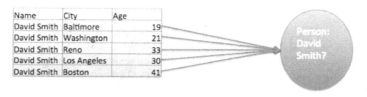

Figure 4.4   Should these David Smiths be represented as one person?

This would be especially problematic if one David Smith has a criminal history, for example, because that criminal history would be shown for all David Smiths in the data. It doesn't quite work even for phone numbers. Imagine our list of students and teachers (in tables 4.1–4.4) was much longer, and two happened to share a common phone number. The visualization would show the student and teacher linked to the same phone, but it doesn't necessarily mean they were sharing a phone; that number could have been given up and later recycled. This problem is called *identity resolution* or *record linkage* and has a history going back many decades. It can become even more complex than described. You may want to merge multiple records under a single node even if none of the properties are an exact match; imagine the situation in table 4.5.

Table 4.5   Three different ways to display data about David Smith. The matching birthdays indicate it's probably the same David Smith, but it's hard for an automated process to understand this because none of the fields match.

Name	DOB
David Smith	10/22/77
D. Smith	22-Oct-77
Smith, David	October 22, 1977

In this case, the records are likely referring to the same person, but the fields all have different text in them, making it difficult for an algorithm to make that determination. There are entire classes of software designed to help with this problem, but it's important to understand the limitations when it comes to graph visualization.

You don't want to have multiple nodes that represent the same thing, because patterns will be missed, but even worse is to think a pattern exists when one doesn't because records were improperly merged. Imagine denying a mortgage to David Smith because you think he has 15 credit cards in default when there are actually 15 different David Smiths!

4.2.2 *Identifying links*

In the previous section, we went through how to identify nodes in our data, either records in a table, such as the students and teachers from tables 4.1–4.4, or a common property such as the phone numbers. They're usually either entire tables or unique instances of one or more properties of a record, but how about links? What defines when one node is linked to another? Sometimes you're lucky, and there's a specific link table in your database, like with the student registrations. Each record in the table represents a link between the student and the class to indicate that the

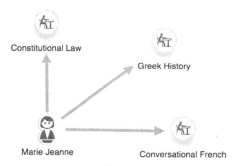

Figure 4.5 The graph representation of Marie Jeanne's classes

student is registered in that class. The result would look something like the diagram in figure 4.5.

But other times, you need to infer a link as opposed to having it explicitly defined in a table. Two nodes that appear in the same record can be the basis for a link between them. In the previous data, if we had decided to make phones a node, then each teacher and each student would be linked to their phone number, and as a result, two students or teachers using the same phone number would stand out on the chart. Sometimes a single row of a table might contain many nodes—imagine a person table that contains details about a person, their address, phone number, spouse's name, and so on. Each one of those might be a separate node, or they could be properties of the original person. The same goes for key-value stores; if two keys share the same value in different records, that can be the basis to draw a link between them.

Then we need to decide what to do with multiple links. If a table has more than one record that links a student to a phone number, is this multiple different relationships or multiple instances of the same relationship? In some cases, it's the former. If we're looking at the email communications from the Enron example in chapter 1, each record represents an email between executives at Enron, and it's an important distinction to know whether two people emailed each other once or hundreds of times.

But other times, it's just duplicate information. In the example of the students and the teachers, a teacher either is teaching a class or is not—it doesn't matter how many times the database reports that information—so a single link would suffice. There's also the case of directed links, which are represented by the arrowheads in figure 4.3. Sometimes a link from A to B means something different than a link from B to A. If I email you, that's different than you emailing me, but the link between a teacher and a class doesn't have that same reversible meaning.

Link directions

There are three main ways of modeling data with multiple relationships in data sets: single, directed, and multiple.

Single—All instances of this relationship should be combined into a single link on the graph, no matter how many times it occurs. This is useful for on/off-type relationships where the only distinction is whether a link exists or not.

Directed—All instances of this relationship, in a specific direction, should be combined—but not combined with links going in the opposite direction. If we're looking at a financial network, maybe it's relevant that I transferred money to you and that you also transferred money back to me, but we're not interested in how many transactions there are between us.

Multiple—All instances in the data of links between two nodes should be represented separately. This is important when each link between the two nodes represents a separate relationship. If I'm looking at an IMDB-type data set with actors and actresses in a movie, and somebody was both an actor and a director in a movie, that's relevant information, and I would want to see two links on my graph.

4.3   *Graph databases*

So far in this chapter, we've been looking at how to model different types of data stores as a graph. There is, however, a data storage format that doesn't require any modeling: the graph database. This section briefly introduces graph databases and talks about how they can be very useful, but not necessary, for graph visualization.

In an effort to capitalize on the increase in popularity of graphs over the past 15 years or so, developers have designed a number of databases specifically to support graphs. The main value of these databases is that the physical model matches—or at least comes close to matching—the logical model. That means there's no complex modeling task required; from the start, all data is stored as nodes, edges, or properties, so you never have to retrofit your data into these categories. The other benefit is that you can ask complex questions about what's connected to what else without extremely complex queries. For example, "What's the name of the class attended by everybody except Toby Quenton, and who teaches it?" To formulate this query in SQL would require joining every single table together, because each piece of requested data lies in a different table. But a graph database, because it stores the items natively in the node-link-property format, doesn't have the complexity or performance limitations of doing indexing lookups for each item. Although that may not make much difference in a four-table database, imagine a multilayered query like this: "Find me all the blue cars with the letter *P* in their license plate owned by registered sex offenders living within two blocks of a library in Palm Beach County." This is called a *graph traversal query* and is one of the main benefits of a graph database. If you're going to be digging deep into complex data on a regular basis, you'll want to use a graph database. There are many different graph databases, both commercial and open source, on the market. I'll highlight two of the most popular here and show you their most useful capabilities.

4.3.1 Neo4j

There are entire books on Neo4j because it's one of the most popular graph databases. It has both a community edition, which is open source, and an enterprise edition that's licensed commercially. Neo4j is produced by Neo Technologies and has been around since 2007. It accepts data in the property graph model, so it has a list of nodes and their properties and a list of edges and their properties. The Neo4j graph database includes its own graph query language (Cypher), a developer workbench environment, and a basic visualization tool known as the Neo4j browser, as shown in figure 4.6.

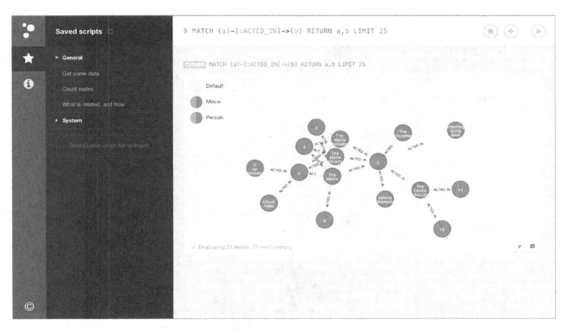

Figure 4.6 The graph visualization component built into Neo4j. It's useful for a quick view of the data you're importing or to preview the results of Cypher queries.

The main method of interacting with Neo4j is with an ASCII art–inspired query language it calls Cypher, a pattern-matching language designed specifically for Neo4j. Here's an example of a Cypher query on the sample data set that comes with the community edition of Neo4j:

```
MATCH (m:Movie)<-[r:ACTED_IN]-(a:Person)
WHERE a.name = 'Keanu Reeves'
RETURN *
```

CYPHER   is the query language for interacting with a Neo4j database. It contains clauses for graph traversal using MATCH or selecting items based on the pattern of links in addition to specific WHERE clauses like traditional SQL. Individual nodes and links can also be added to the Neo4j database via CREATE statements, although Neo4j has bulk import tools for adding large amounts of data that are more efficient than individual CREATE statements for each record.

What appears after the MATCH statement is the pattern we want to match. This is all movies that have actors or actresses: m is a variable name, and m:Movie means "match all nodes of type movie." The <-- string indicates a link, in this case a directed one showing that we're looking for links pointing toward the movie. We're looking only for links of a particular type though, so interjected in the link symbol is [r:ACTED_IN], meaning if there are also links for stagehands or directors, we don't want to find those. Then the other side of the link must be a node of type person.

The WHERE clause is similar to how it works in SQL—it restricts the output to that which satisfies the condition set, in this case, only actors named 'Keanu Reeves'. The RETURN statement can be useful to restrict which items we want returned from the query, but in this case, we want to see everything. Thus, we use an asterisk, *, to tell this to Neo4j.

When pasted into the Neo4j browser, we get the result shown in figure 4.7: a basic visualization of Keanu and some of his movies.

Figure 4.7   The Neo4j browser's result of all movies linked to Keanu Reeves, created using Cypher

For more-complex visualizations, Neo4j can work with both Gephi and KeyLines. For Gephi, you can get a plugin here: https://marketplace.gephi.org/plugin/neo4j-graph-database-support/.

This allows Gephi to read directly from the database files that Neo4j uses to do much of the graph manipulation that you saw in chapter 3 directly on a Neo4j data set.

For KeyLines, Neo4j includes a REST (Representational State Transfer—a technology for interacting with server applications via URLs) endpoint that allows submission of a Cypher query via HTTP POST and returns the results as a JSON object. As you learned in chapter 3, KeyLines consumes JSON to create its visualization, but the two formats aren't quite the same, so some translation needs to be done in JavaScript to get the data in the right format for display in KeyLines; an example follows. This isn't a complete application, although it can be merged with the source example in chapter 3 or downloaded from the KeyLines site:

```
function sendQuery (query, callback) {          Send an Ajax call
  $.ajax({                                      with jQuery library
    type: 'POST',
    url:'http://localhost:7474/db/data/transaction/commit',   The default
    data: JSON.stringify(query),                URL for the
    headers: {                                  Neo4j Cypher
      Authorization: 'Basic '+btoa('dbUsername:dbPassword')   endpoint
    },
    dataType: 'json',                           Security check:
    contentType: 'application/json'             Neo4j wants
  })                                            login credentials
.done(callback)                                 alongside each
}                                               query, passed
                                                here
```

Then we need to parse through the items that Neo4j returns and make KeyLines JSON from them:

```
function makeKeyLinesItems(json){               Populate this with
  var items = [];                               our KeyLines JSON

  $.each(json.results[0].data, function (i, entry){   Iterate through
                                                      each node in the
    $.each(entry.graph.nodes, function (j, node){     Neo4j return and
                                                      call a function
      var node = makeNode(node);                      called makeNode
      items.push(node);                               to assemble
                                                      KeyLines JSON
    });
    $.each(entry.graph.relationships, function (j, edge){   Do the same
                                                            thing with links
      var link = makeLink(edge);                            and push both
      items.push(link);                                     to array

    });

  });

  return items;
}
```

Finally, we'll write those `makeNode` and `makeLink` functions to take an item in the returns, look at its properties, and create the appropriate KeyLines JSON:

```
function makeNode(item) {
  var baseType = getType(item.labels);
  var label = item.properties.name;
  return {
    id: item.id,
    type: 'node',
    t: label,
    u: getNodeIcon(baseType),
    ci: true,
    e: baseType === 'movie' ? 2 : 1,
    d: item
  };
}

function makeLink(item) {
  var id = item.id + ':' + item.startNode + '-' + item.endNode;
  var labels = item.properties.roles;

  return {
    type: 'link',
    id1: item.startNode,
    id2: item.endNode,
    id: id,
    t: labels ? labels.join(' ') : '',
    fc: 'rgba(52,52,52,0.9)',
    a2: true,
    c: 'rgb(0,153,255)',
    w: 2,
    d: item
  };
}
```

Annotations:
- **Allows you to use appropriate icon for either movies or actors**
- **Take name property and use it as the label on the node**
- **Pass the URL of appropriate node icon**
- **e stands for "enlargement," making the movie nodes twice the size of the actor ones**
- **The d property in KeyLines is special; it allows you to store any data alongside the node or link.**
- **id1 and id2 properties refer to IDs of the endpoints of the link**
- **KeyLines requires an id property that's unique among both nodes and links, as opposed to Neo4j, which has a separate id field for nodes or links, so we need to create something unique here.**
- **Add an arrowhead from the actor to the movie; this will show the results of the Cypher query as a KeyLines chart in the web page.**

4.3.2   *Titan*

Another popular software option is Titan, an open source, graph database written by Aurelius and now community supported, because Aurelius itself was purchased by DataStax. Unlike Neo4j, it was designed with scale in mind; there are production implementations of Titan with hundreds of billions of nodes and edges. Although performance in Neo4j has recently improved, I still hear from my clients that Titan outperforms Neo4j on large data sets. Also unlike Neo4j, Titan doesn't have a proprietary database backend; it allows you to choose a scalable backend like Apache Cassandra or Apache HBase. This allows you to distribute the server workload and storage across many different machines.

Interaction with a Titan database is done via the *TinkerPop* stack, an open source framework for working with graph databases. TinkerPop is complex enough to be the subject of its own book, so here we'll just address a few components. First is the query language included as part of TinkerPop, *Gremlin*.

GREMLIN is the query language for TinkerPop, the open source, graph framework that works on top of Titan as well as some other graph databases. It's Titan's equivalent of Cypher, though unlike Cypher, it's language-dependent—implementations exist for Java and Groovy, among others.

Here's an example Gremlin query, designed to be equivalent to the previous Cypher query. Note that the Gremlin terminology uses *vertex* to mean *node* and *edge* to mean *link*:

```
gremlin> g.V("name","Keanu Reeves")
==> v[1]
gremlin> v[1].outE.has("type","ACTED_IN").outV.name

==> "Point Break"
==> "The Matrix"
==> "Speed"
```

> g defines the entire graph; here we search for a vertex (node) with the name property set to Keanu Reeves.

> outE gets the outbound edges from vertex I, the Keanu Reeves node. Here we look for only those edges with the type property set to ACTED_IN. outV gets the vertex at the other end of the edge, in this case, the movies that Keanu has acted in.

Like Neo4j, Titan can be visualized in both Gephi and KeyLines. The Gremlin query language has a function to save the graph to GraphML, a specialized XML format for saving graphs:

```
g.saveGraphML('movies.graphml');
```

This will save a file in the GraphML format, which can then be opened with Gephi.

To connect KeyLines to Titan, we'll take advantage of another tool in the Tinker-Pop stack that lets us interact with Titan through REST, similar to the way we worked with Neo4j. This is called Rexster, and it allows us to make Ajax calls from our JavaScript to pass Gremlin queries directly to Titan and get the results back in JSON. The JavaScript code would look something like the following:

```
function callRexster(query, callback) {
  $.ajax({
    type: 'GET',
    url: rexsterURL+query,
    dataType: 'json',
    contentType: 'application/json',
    success: function (json) {
      console.log(json);
      var items = [];

      forEach(json.results, function (item) {
        if(item._type === 'vertex'){
          items.push(createNode(item));
        } else {
          items.push(createLink(item));
        }
      });
    });

    callback(items);
```

> Use jQuery library to make an Ajax call to Rexster endpoint

> URL for the REST endpoint for Rexster and text of Gremlin query would be combined in this line

> Cycle through each item in the return, both vertices and edges, and create appropriate KeyLines JSON object with the visual properties

This block of code calls two functions, `createNode` and `createLink`, that get called for each node or link in the data returned from Titan. Those functions aren't written out here because they would be nearly identical to the `makeNode` and `makeLink` functions from the Neo4j example.

4.4   Summary

In this chapter, we talked about data modeling—how you take data in various formats and represent it as nodes and links. This is an important step to creating graph visualization. Now that you understand how to get data into your visualization, in the next chapter we'll discuss how to make visualizations useful and intuitive.

- A model is a logical view that can either closely map the physical structure of the database or be quite removed from it.
- Many different models of the same database are possible; some may be more useful than others.
- A graph model defines nodes, links, and properties, and can be made from data originally stored in relational or schema-less databases.
- Graph databases store the data in a graph model natively, so no modeling is required.
- Many graph database technologies are available. Neo4j and Titan are two of the most popular, and data from these sources can be visualized in Gephi or KeyLines.

How to build
graph visualizations

This chapter covers
- Designing graphics with your user in mind
- Using visual properties to represent data on a graph
- Using size and color
- Styling links
- Determining how much data to put on the graph

Because graph data analytics, data visualization, and data modeling are technical subjects, often performed by data scientists, engineers, and application developers, the design of the information and how it's presented to the end user are often an afterthought. This is disappointing, because a poorly designed visualization can often derail the entire project. Take a look at the graph in figure 5.1 from NodeXL (the full-color one is available in the eBook and here: http://mng.bz/2iy7).

This is an attempt to show the relationships among Twitter comments on a *New York Times* article about anti-Muslim bigotry, but there's way too much clutter. It's not clear why it's segmented into separate boxes, and the nodes all overlap one another, making a mostly useless diagram of what could be interesting data. If end

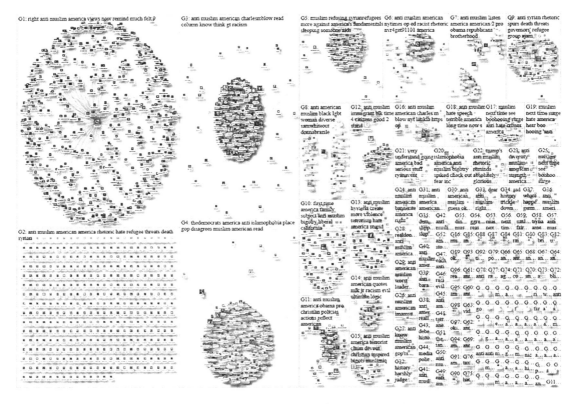

Figure 5.1   An unhelpful graph visualization because of poor design

users don't intuitively and immediately understand what they're looking at and why, they're unlikely to use the data in any meaningful way. This chapter talks about design principles for data in general. Data-visualization pioneer Edward Tufte's book *Envisioning Information* (Graphics Press, 1990) is the bible for general data visualization, and we'll draw heavily on his design principles, applying them specifically to graph data.

5.1   *Understanding your user*

The first question to ask yourself when designing a graph is, "Who will be my end user?" A graph designed for data scientists who are intimately familiar with the structure and contents of the data should look quite different from one designed for the CEO who's making corporate investment decisions based on the data. Figures 5.2 and 5.3 show two graphs presenting the same data, one optimized for a technical audience and one designed for a business audience.

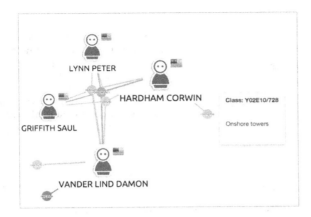

Figure 5.2   Using visual properties such as glyphs to show collaborators on patents

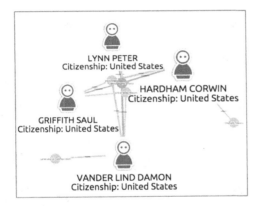

Figure 5.3   Using labels to explain the nodes and edges in more detail

In these figures, the graph for the nontechnical audience uses visual cues to *explain* the data, whereas the technical one uses visual cues to *describe* the data. The first example shows the properties of the people in the labels alongside the property name, and the second diagram uses the visual properties of the nodes, such as size and color, to convey those same properties. Although this is harder to understand for someone unfamiliar with the data, certain values will immediately stand out without the benefit of the text of each label. In addition, graphs for an unsophisticated audience should minimize the number of node types used because the less familiar your audience is with the data, the harder it will be for them to immediately grasp the significance of the size of a node or the width of an edge. Instead of showing two people linked to the same family node, show a link directly between them indicating the familial relationship, as shown in figure 5.4.

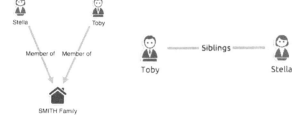

Figure 5.4   Removing unnecessary node types by linking items directly together. Here, the diagram on the right can actually convey more information. The diagram on the left just tells us that Toby and Stella are part of the same family, whereas the one on the right shows that they're siblings.

Audience-based visual design

The following list has some pointers on which visual features can be the most useful, depending on your audience.

Sophisticated audience:

- Visual properties convey data properties on both nodes and links.
- Use minimal labels.
- Add a legend to describe the property mappings.
- Employ more node types.

Unsophisticated audience:

- Provide more information on labels.
- Use node icons to convey type.
- A legend shouldn't be necessary.
- Employ fewer node types.

5.2   *Using intuitive visual properties*

Graph visualizations are as much art as science. You're aiming to create an understanding of the data in your viewer's mind, but simply plotting identical nodes and links fails to take full advantage of the visual processing faculties in the viewer's brain. In addition to reading text, people are hardwired to recognize sizes and colors instantly, and those visual clues will stand out to a graph viewer much more significantly than text. See table 5.1 for a list of visual properties and when they should be used.

Table 5.1   Visual properties and when they're helpful

Size	Useful for scalar properties.
	Should convey a property related to size.
	Be careful about scale (for example, logarithmic scales can be useful).
Color	Useful for group membership.
	Not good for gradients.
	Both nodes and links can be colored.

Table 5.1 Visual properties and when they're helpful *(continued)*

Node icons	Useful to show the type of node. Can also be used to show an image of the actual item being depicted (such as a photo of the person).
Glyphs	Attach a property to a node or link visually. Limit to one or maybe two glyphs. Images are best but short bits of text are OK.
Labels	Short node labels are OK, but avoid anything longer than a couple of words. Avoid labels on links unless necessary for understanding the relationship. Consider showing link labels on hover or click.

5.2.1 Size

Consider the diagram in figure 5.5. Here, I use the size of the node to indicate the population of each US state. See how it's immediately obvious what the most populous states are in this visualization.

Figure 5.5 The states represented in the graph, sized according to their population

Here, I use a linear mapping, so the California node, with a population of 37 million, is almost seven times larger than the Wisconsin node, with a population of 5.6 million. This works well and is intuitive when the values are within an order of magnitude of each other but is not realistic when the values vary significantly more than that. For example, if I had nodes representing the entire United States (population 308 million) and my household (population 4), there's no way to draw one node millions of times larger than another. In a case like that, a logarithmic scale, where each doubling in size represents a 10-times greater property value, may make more sense. You can bind the node size property to any value you like, but your viewers are going to implicitly assume that node size corresponds to some property indicating larger amounts or importance. Looking at the previous diagram, you might initially believe the states are sized according to their land mass, except you know that Alaska is four times the size of California in square mileage. Your brain then looks for some other way to make sense of the data. But size is less helpful if bound to a ratio, such as something like GDP per capita, or an intangible quality, such as a measure of health. For those types of measures, using color makes more sense.

5.2.2   *Color*

Color is useful for properties that fall into discrete buckets, not properties that scale. Although it's possible to scale colors—for example, RGB (Red, Green, Blue) values of (0,0,0) to (255,0,0) will scale from black to primary red—it's difficult for a user to discern subtle differences in color. In figure 5.6, I've taken the graph from figure 5.5 and scaled the nodes from light gray to black to indicate population density.

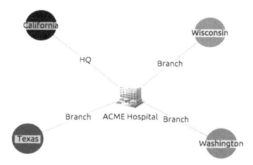

Figure 5.6   You can tell that Washington and Wisconsin are a lighter gray than California or Texas, but the individual differences are hard to see.

Much better is to use discrete colors to indicate group membership. The graph in figure 5.7 is internal emails (anonymized) that I collected from a technology company. I selected a separate color for each department within the company, as shown in the legend. (In the print edition of this book, this figure is reproduced in the center color section.)

By using the colors to indicate group membership—in this case, the employee's department—trends become more apparent, because it's easy to spot the same colors across the chart. For example, in figure 5.7, notice the tech employees Nicholas and Christopher at the right side of the chart. They aren't connected to the other techies; they communicate only through a salesperson. Odd, right? That suggests perhaps they are offsite or are otherwise isolated from the rest of the company's tech team.

Links can have colors and sizing as well, and this can be a powerful way to convey information about the relationship between the nodes. In figure 5.7, the link using the department coding is colored if the email is internal to that department (if both the sender and receiver are members of that department). For external communication,

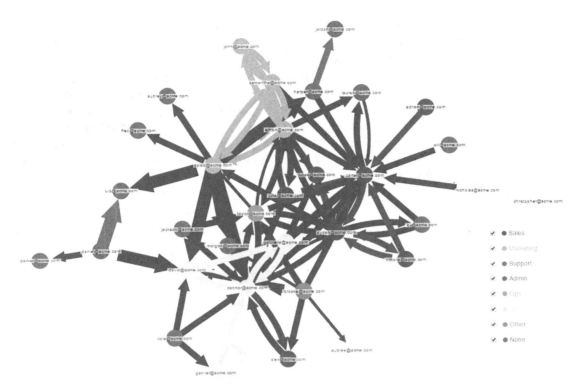

Figure 5.7   A graph of internal emails within a technology company. Nodes are color-coded by department so that it's easy to see group membership at a glance and notice broad trends across departments. This diagram is included in the color section in the print edition of this book.

the edge is black. The way to show size on a link is with the link width, and just like with node sizing, the user will assume that a thick link between two nodes indicates a stronger relationship than a thin one, so link width should be assigned to a property that correlates with the strength of the relationship. In figure 5.8, the link width is assigned to the volume of emails between those individuals, so thick lines link people who communicate a lot, and thinner lines show fewer emails between those employees.

Figure 5.8   The thick link at the top implies a stronger relationship between the nodes than the thin link at the bottom.

Although sizing and coloring can be powerful visual cues to create an understanding of data, it's possible to get too clever. A viewer can really only hold in their head two variables at once, so presenting a graph of people that scales the size of the node with the person's age, the color of the node with their height, and the color of the border with their weight would not be helpful. The viewer would constantly be wondering, "OK, what does a red border mean again?"

The biggest mistake you could make would be independently controlling the RGB values and assigning them to different properties. Could you imagine a graph with the red value assigned to property A, green assigned to property B, and blue assigned to property C? This would mean that a yellow item was high in A and B but low in C. A cyan item would be high in B and C, but low in A. I've seen this before and it was every bit as terrible as it sounds. It's far clearer to bind property A to the size of the node and property B to the color of the node.

5.2.3   *Node icons*

Look at the difference in the two figures from earlier in the chapter, as shown in figure 5.9.

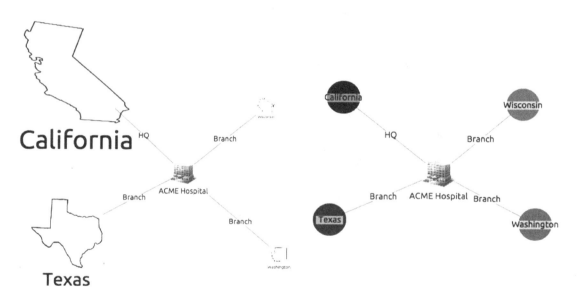

Figure 5.9   Nodes as shapes versus icons

In the first example, I used the state outline to represent that state on the graph, so California looks like California, whereas in the second figure, nodes are generic circles. Three possibilities for how to represent nodes on the graph are shown in figure 5.10, and each has its advantages and disadvantages: shapes, individual representations, and type representations.

Type Representation

Individual Representation

Figure 5.10   The three types of node representations

Type representation is the most useful. In this case, you assign an icon representing the class of nodes to which each node belongs. For all nodes that represent a person, you show a generic person icon. For all nodes that represent a vehicle, you show a vehicle icon. This is helpful because a viewer doesn't have to read any text to figure out what they're looking at.

Individual representations can be useful if you have a visual representation of the individual node, such as a photograph for each person. This can be most helpful when you're working with social media data because typically all the nodes are people. Using type representation for every node misses out on an opportunity to give more detail because every node will look alike. And typically when working with social media data, you almost always have access to photos of people uploaded by the persons themselves (see the Twitter example in chapter 2).

Generic shapes can also be useful, especially if you want to use color to show a property, as indicated in the previous section. It may be more helpful to use border colors, even with icons or photos, as shown in figure 5.11.

Type Representation

Individual Representation

Shape

Figure 5.11   The three core node representation types with blue borders. Borders can be used sparingly to indicate a color property, even with photos or icons.

Occasionally, a pie-chart node representation can be helpful when your nodes represent groups of objects, and you'd like to show the user the breakdown of items in that group. For example, the chart in figure 5.12 represents the proportion of morning versus evening subscribers of the newspapers owned by a media company.

Figure 5.12   Nodes resemble pie charts to display a quick glance at the individual items that compose each node.

But this is less helpful with charts larger than a dozen nodes because they get very busy and difficult to read, especially if you have more than two or three colors on each node.

5.2.4   *Glyphs*

Another way of annotating nodes is to use glyphs, which are basically ornaments on the node presenting the viewer with the value of one or more additional properties on the node right on the surface of the chart. A glyph augments the node representation, as discussed previously, and can take the form of either an image or text. Figure 5.13 shows an example of a text-based glyph to display the age of each person or pet in a family.

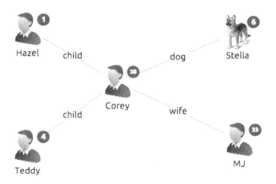

Figure 5.13   A text-based glyph indicating the ages of the members of my family

Sometimes image-based glyphs can also be useful. For example, perhaps some nodes should have a warning symbol attached to them so that when the viewer sees them, they know to be careful. This has several different applications. It could be life saving for law enforcement to flag which criminals have prior violent crime convictions or

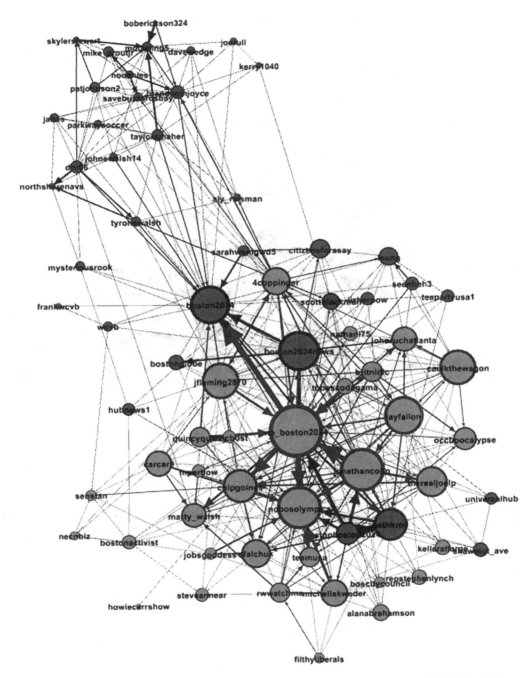

Figure 3.9   The social graph of people tweeting about the Boston Olympics bid for 2024 in Gephi. I used community detection to help color nodes by their support of or opposition to the bid.

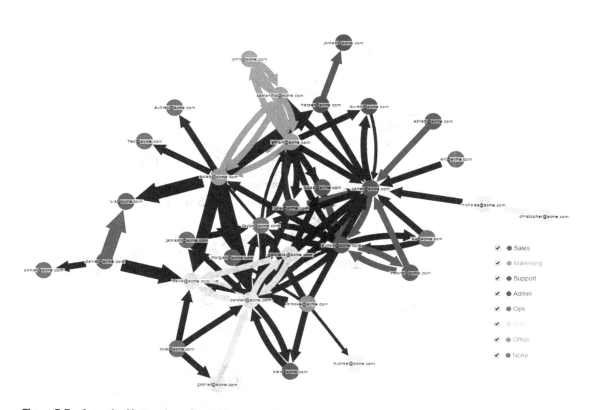

Figure 5.7 A graph of internal emails within a technology company. Nodes are color-coded by department so that it's easy to see group membership at a glance and notice broad trends across departments.

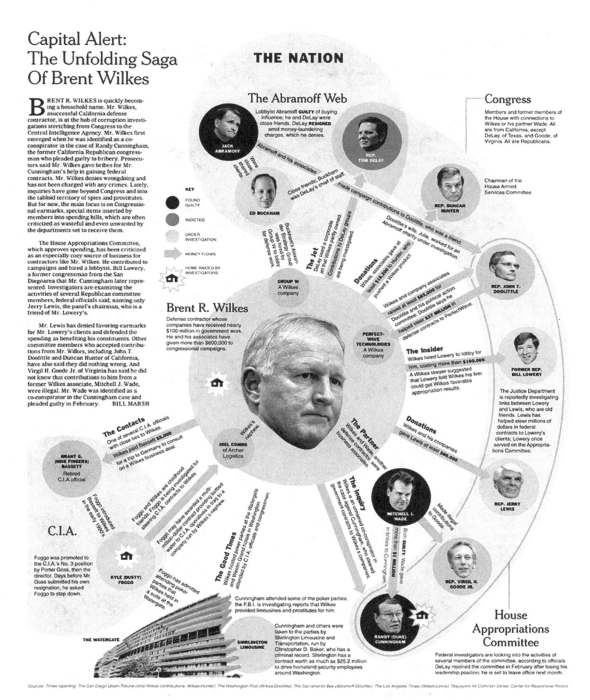

Figure 5.16   A graph of the interaction among lobbyists, members of Congress, and bribes in both the Jack Abramoff and Duke Cunningham bribery scandals (originally published in the *New York Times*).

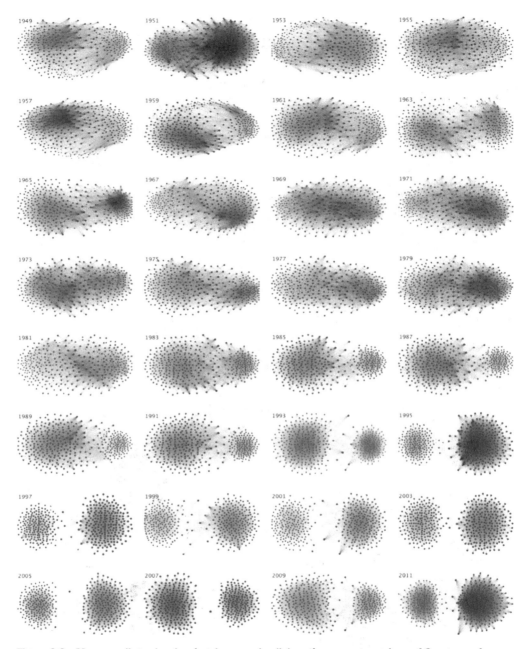

Figure 9.3 Many small graphs showing decreased collaboration among members of Congress of different parties over time. Look at the difference between the 1993 makeup of Congress and 1995: many more Republicans were elected, and it marked a shift to the time when collaboration between the parties has all but ended.

simply useful for IT departments to identify which servers are currently malfunctioning. Or a flag can indicate the country of origin, which is more elegant than text, as you can see in figure 5.14.

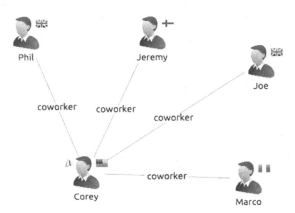

Figure 5.14 **The citizenship of my coworkers, as shown through glyphs. The Corey node also has a warning symbol attached to it; you could design a graph visualization to enable you to hover your mouse over the glyph for further information, which is explained in more detail in chapter 6.**

Glyphs are helpful for bits of data that your viewers need to know after identifying a specific node, but they're less helpful when the user wants to identify nodes sharing a common property. Scanning the chart for all the Italian flags would be a challenge, and perhaps color would be a better visual cue in that case.

5.2.5 Labels

Labels can be useful in small doses but tricky to get right. You want enough text on the nodes so that the viewer can identify what they are looking at, but not so much that it clutters the chart and makes it hard to understand. A chart with no labels on the nodes is just a pretty picture, as shown in figure 5.15, because no discernible information can be gleaned from it; but labels can often be omitted from links altogether.

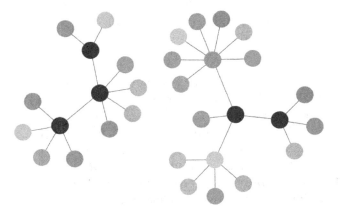

Figure 5.15 **A chart with no labels is just a pretty picture and not helpful.**

A good rule of thumb is that the label on a node should be the shortest bit of text that allows the viewer to identify the node, and it should be human readable. This means that you should use names instead of identification numbers, for example, or car makes and models instead of VINs. The value on the label needn't be (and often shouldn't be) the identifier of that node in the chart. Think back to chapter 4, where we were discussing identity resolution. You don't want "John Smith" to be the unique identifier of a node on a chart or else every "John Smith" in your data will be merged into one node. You want to use something like John's Social Security number. But an SSN is not a human-readable number. Nobody recognizes someone from their SSN, so the label of the node should instead be the name. There's no problem having multiple nodes on the chart with the same label.

Labels on the links often add no value, but occasionally it's important to label the type of the relationship. For example, John and Jerry are brothers, whereas Jerry and Phil are business partners. You can also easily illustrate this with link colors, creating less clutter on the chart. Avoid automatically adding the relationship type as the label of the link, especially when it's obvious. A corporate hierarchy chart doesn't need every link to say "reports to," for instance.

5.3   *Building charts with visual properties*

You now have an overview of the main design principles of data visualization. The next section shows you how to implement these design principles using KeyLines and Gephi. The chart in figure 5.16 was hand-drawn in the *New York Times* in 2006, and I'll refer to it several times in the rest of the book. The figure is in grayscale in the print book; you can see the full-color version in the colored insert of this book.

Look at some of the visual properties that the *Times* decided to use—how many can you see? Are they well designed? The node icon shows a photo of the person involved, the node size determines the node's relative importance in the scandal, and the color indicates whether that person was convicted. A glyph on the node indicates whether that person was the subject of an FBI raid. This is a very good design, though I'd argue that there's far too much text on the link labels. This is one of the limitations of a print diagram, which we'll explore in chapter 6. Let's look at how a chart like this would be defined in both KeyLines and Gephi.

KEYLINES

Any graph visualization software worth its salt will allow you to customize your data using the principles outlined in the previous section. I've used KeyLines to produce most of the example images in this chapter. I'll show you how to create a visual like the Abramoff chart in KeyLines. KeyLines publishes a JSON data format as part of its SDK, which allows you to specify the visual properties of the data you want to present in the visualization. For example, following is a snippet of the JSON specification of the chart of the Abramoff chart as represented in KeyLines. The full JSON can be downloaded from http://cambridge-intelligence.com/visualizing-graph-data/.

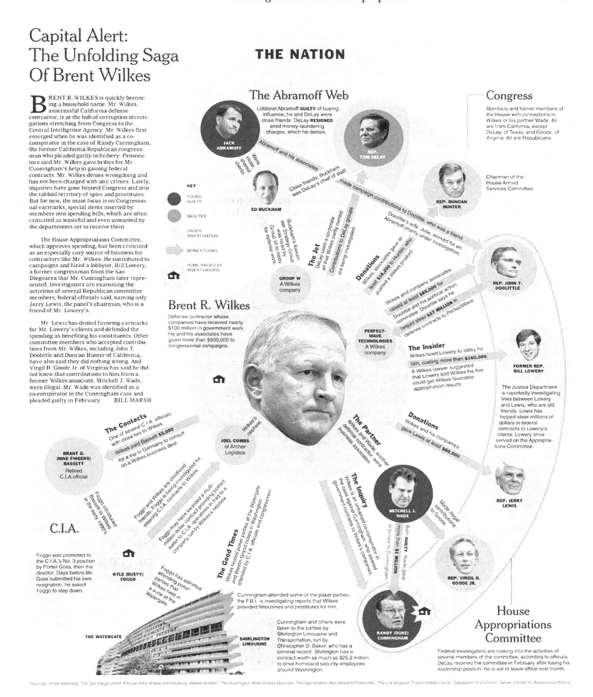

Figure 5.16 A graph of the interaction among lobbyists, members of Congress, and bribes in both the Jack Abramoff and Duke Cunningham bribery scandals (Bill Marsh, "The Abramoff Web," *New York Times*, May 21, 2006)

```
{
  "type": "LinkChart",
  "items": [
    {
      "c": "rgb(255, 127, 127)",          ◁──  Color of the link
      "t": "",                             ◁──  Text of the link label
      "w": 5,                              ◁──  Width of the link
      "a2": true,                          ◁──  Whether there's an
      "id": "15",                               arrowhead or not
      "id1": "1",
      "id2": "14",                         ◁──  The two end
      "type": "link",                           points of the link
      "off": 0
    },                                     ◁──  A type to determine
    {                                           whether this is a node
      "type": "node",                           or a link
      "id": "5",
      "u": "images/itemstyles/person2.png", ◁── URL of the node icon
      "x": 873.6051023252265,              ◁──  Location of the node
      "y": 102.9183104440354,                   in x,y coordinates
      "t": "Kyle (Dusty) Foggo",           ◁──  Text of the label
      "fs": "",
      "fc": "",
      "fbc": "",
      "sh": "circle",
      "ci": false,
      "e": 1,
      "c": "yellow",                       ◁──  Background color,
      "ha": [],                                 yellow in this case
      "g": [
        {
          "p": "ne",
          "u": "images/itemstyles/Home-icon.png"  ◁── URL of the home
        }                                              raid glyph
      ]
    },
  }
```

Identifier that uniquely determines the link

In an effort to minimize bandwidth, the property names are short abbreviations—the documentation must be consulted often to look up the property names. In this example, e: stands for "enlargement" where 1 is normal; a node with an e value of 2 is double the normal size. The u: property points to the URL of the image used for either the node icon or the glyph, and it can be a PNG or a JPG file. The t: property stands for "text" and is used as the text label for either the node or the glyph. The c: property on a node or glyph allows you to define the color using RGB values. The g: property stands for "glyphs" and is an array of JSON objects defining the visual properties of the glyphs. KeyLines lacks the ability to show pie charts as nodes. In addition, all properties have to be set manually or algorithmically when building the JSON, so scaling them to a range of values in the data is a manual process. In the states example, figure 5.5, where I scaled the size of the state nodes according to their population, I had to determine that I wanted a linear scale, assign Wisconsin to size 0.75, and then determine how many "Wisconsins" were in the other states, to find the correct enlargement factor.

The full chart, represented in KeyLines, is shown in figure 5.17.

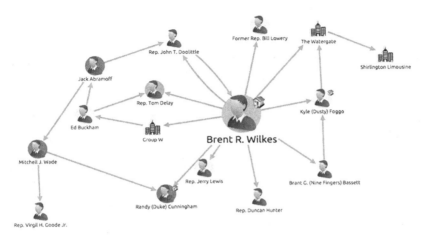

Figure 5.17 The *New York Times* Jack Abramoff chart rendered in KeyLines using the properties identified earlier

GEPHI

In Gephi, we can re-create the Jack Abramoff chart manually by drawing nodes and links or entering them on the Data Laboratory pane of the user interface, as shown in figure 5.18.

Figure 5.18 Typing the names into the Gephi UI

Links can be drawn using the edge pencil tool on the left side of the overview window, as shown in figure 5.19.

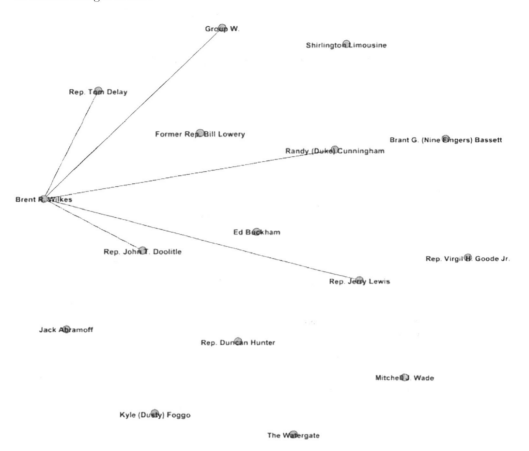

Figure 5.19   Using the edge pencil to draw links

Nodes can then be colored and sized manually by using the brush and size tools, located just above the edge pencil. After doing these steps, we get a Gephi chart that resembles the *New York Times* Abramoff chart, though a little simpler, as shown in figure 5.20.

Figure 5.20   The completed Abramoff chart in Gephi

This is the simplest means of using Gephi, and it's capable of much more automatic determination of visual properties. The sizing and coloring of nodes and links can also be mapped to data properties, and this is done from the Appearance pane, which by default is in the upper-left corner of the Gephi window, as shown in figure 5.21.

Figure 5.21   The Appearance pane in Gephi allows you to customize node and edge sizing and color.

Gephi has changed the way you assign size and color to nodes and links from version 0.8x to version 0.9x. The previous panes Partition and Ranking are now combined and called Appearance. For properties of nodes and links that fall into discrete categories, you take your nodes, partition them into various groups, and assign a color to each group. It's only useful for properties that have fewer than five discrete values, because coloring nodes by group is useless if every node is in a separate group. All the node properties will appear in the drop-down box in figure 5.21. After selecting the appropriate category, you'll see a list of groups, and Gephi will automatically assign a color to each group, but you can change that by clicking the color box at the left of the group, as shown in figure 5.22.

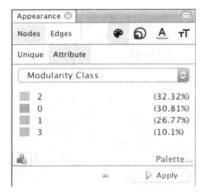

Figure 5.22   The nodes in Gephi separated into four distinct groups and colored that way

For coloring edges, you follow the exact same process.

If the property is a scalar value, Gephi will allow you to size or color nodes by scaling them according to a numeric value. This is also done from the Appearance pane. The process is quite similar. The drop-down will have a list of properties that you've imported for your nodes. To scale by color gradient (the default), select the color wheel on the upper-right corner of the tab. By clicking the color palette on the left, you can select the color gradient that you want. See figure 5.23.

Figure 5.23 Selecting a color gradient for node color schemes in Gephi

The process for sizing nodes or edges is similar, and you can do both in Gephi. Next to the palette icon in figure 5.24 is an icon of three different-size circles. This icon represents dynamic sizing of nodes, and you have a number of options on how that should work, including the maximum and minimum sizes of nodes you'd like to see on the graph and which property ranges should be included. In addition, the Spline tool can be very powerful and is often overlooked. Imagine you had a data set that consisted of dozens of nodes with values all clustering around 50 and one node with a property value of 1. A linear sizing algorithm would show very little difference between any of the nodes except the outlier, which would be dramatically smaller. You may want to highlight the differences between the other values as well and so may opt for a non-linear way of assigning sizes to nodes. I won't go through the dense mathematics here, but for further reference, look up "spline interpolation" on Wikipedia. Figures 5.24 and 5.25 show the details.

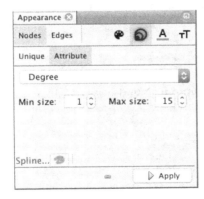

Figure 5.24 Rank node sizes according to the property selected in the drop-down box in Gephi.

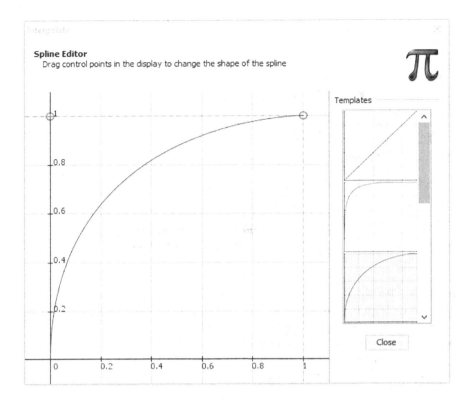

Figure 5.25   Select a linear or non-linear interpolation between the maximum and minimum values associated with node or edge properties. This is useful if you have extremely large or extremely small differences between property values.

Finally, label support is somewhat limited in Gephi. Nodes and edges take their labels from a property in the data table with the name "label," and that's the value that will be shown on the graph when the labels are turned on. The size, font, and font color of the labels can be controlled from the label toolbar, as shown in figure 5.26. The dark *T* turns the labels on or off.

Figure 5.26   The label toolbar in Gephi. The leftmost button turns the labels on or off.

5.4   *Summary*

In this chapter you learned the following:

- The best designs of graph visualizations come from understanding the users and what questions they might have of the data.
- Sophisticated users who understand the data can have data properties bound to visual properties effectively. Unsophisticated users likely need more guidance and text.
- Node sizes are most effective when used to convey a numeric value that acts as a count.
- Link widths are useful for indicating the strength of the relationship between two nodes.
- Colors are rarely effective gradients and are better used to indicate group membership.
- Labels should be informative and human readable and should be minimized on links.
- KeyLines controls these properties through code, specifically, manipulation of the JSON.
- Gephi has a user interface for binding visual properties to data properties.

Creating interactive
visualizations

This chapter covers

- The benefits of dynamic versus static diagrams
- Navigating the chart
- Charting user actions
- Using animation sparingly
- Designing for mobile platforms

Although the earliest graphs were drawn using pencil and paper, modern graph visualization is all done via computer. As a result, the charts being produced don't have to be static images but can change in response to user input. The benefit of interactive visualizations is that you aren't limited to whatever you can print on a page—you can display complex data that users can drill into. A perfect example of this is how a newspaper might use an infographic in its print edition but offer a better interactive graph visualization in its online version of the story. Adding interactivity to a graph allows users to gain a broader and deeper understanding of the data. Let's return to the Abramoff chart that we first encountered in chapter 5, reproduced in figure 6.1.

This chart appeared in both the print and online editions of the *New York Times* in 2006. Although I think this is a well-designed visualization of the complex

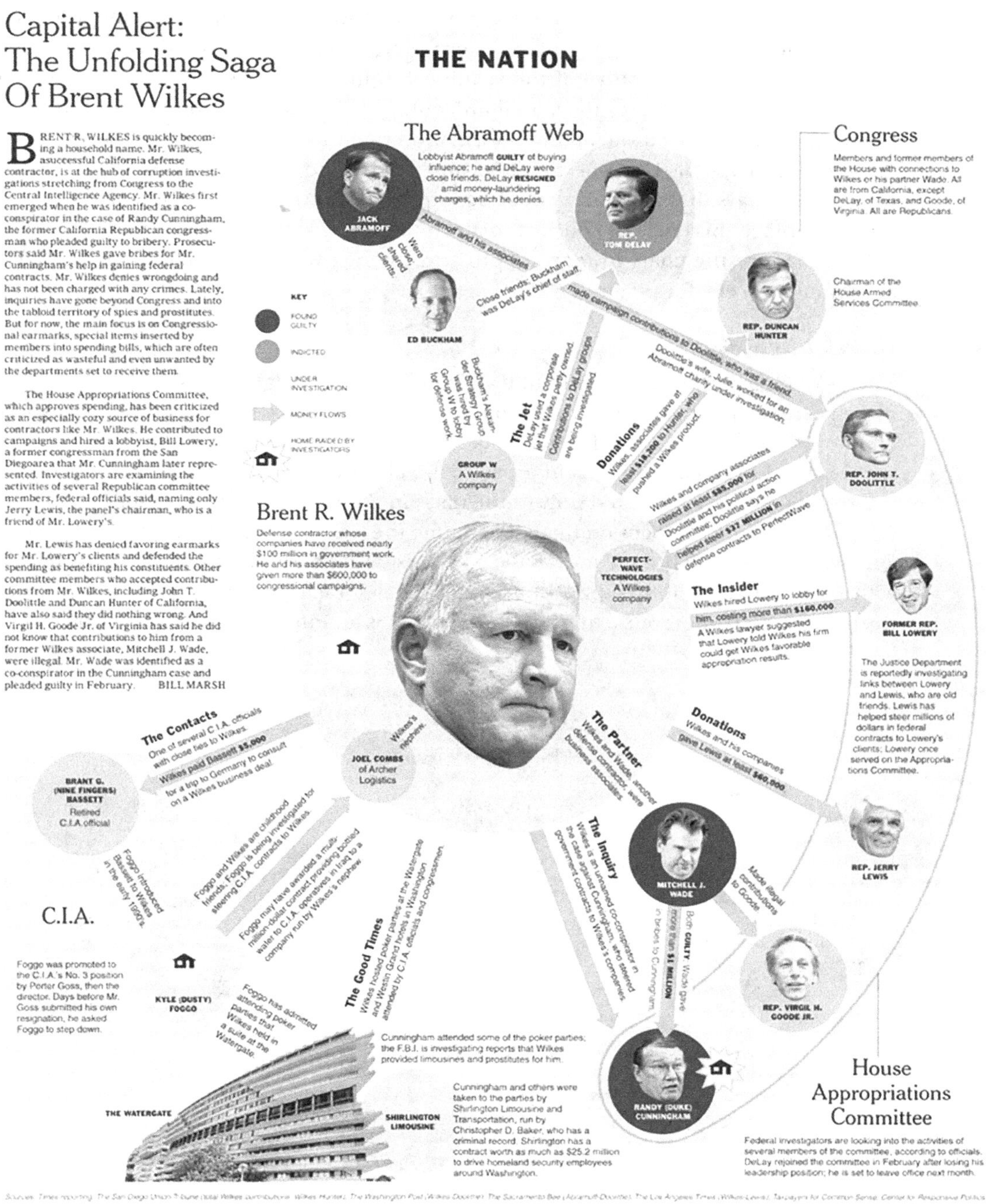

Capital Alert: The Unfolding Saga Of Brent Wilkes

BRENT R. WILKES is quickly becoming a household name. Mr. Wilkes, a successful California defense contractor, is at the hub of corruption investigations stretching from Congress to the Central Intelligence Agency. Mr. Wilkes first emerged when he was identified as a co-conspirator in the case of Randy Cunningham, the former California Republican congressman who pleaded guilty to bribery. Prosecutors said Mr. Wilkes gave bribes for Mr. Cunningham's help in gaining federal contracts. Mr. Wilkes denies wrongdoing and has not been charged with any crimes. Lately, inquiries have gone beyond Congress and into the tabloid territory of spies and prostitutes. But for now, the main focus is on Congressional earmarks, special items inserted by members into spending bills, which are often criticized as wasteful and even unwanted by the departments set to receive them.

The House Appropriations Committee, which approves spending, has been criticized as an especially cozy source of business for contractors like Mr. Wilkes. He contributed to campaigns and hired a lobbyist, Bill Lowery, a former congressman from the San Diego area that Mr. Cunningham later represented. Investigators are examining the activities of several Republican committee members, federal officials said, naming only Jerry Lewis, the panel's chairman, who is a friend of Mr. Lowery's.

Mr. Lewis has denied favoring earmarks for Mr. Lowery's clients and defended the spending as benefiting his constituents. Other committee members who accepted contributions from Mr. Wilkes, including John T. Doolittle and Duncan Hunter of California, have also said they did nothing wrong. And Virgil H. Goode Jr. of Virginia has said he did not know that contributions to him from a former Wilkes associate, Mitchell J. Wade, were illegal. Mr. Wade was identified as a co-conspirator in the Cunningham case and pleaded guilty in February.   BILL MARSH

Figure 6.1   Revisiting the Abramoff chart

interactions among Congress, defense contractors, and other companies, I mentioned a few quibbles in chapter 5. First of all, there's too much text on the links; the author tries to describe the narrative of the relationship in the link itself, which takes up so much space that it obscures the actual link entirely. This is a consequence of the print medium of the visualization: all the information that the author wants to convey needs to be on the page at the same time, because there's no interactivity. In this chapter, we'll look at ways that this chart could be improved by creating an interactive application to explore this data. In contrast to a printed page, a digital application allows the user to explore the chart in more depth and interact with it via clicks, double-clicks, and mouse hovers, for example.

6.1   *Chart navigation*

The most basic way to allow a user to learn more about the data is to allow navigation of the chart, mostly with panning and zooming. By enabling zooming, users can inspect areas of detail that would be hard to make out at full scale, and panning allows users to see this level of detail in different areas of the chart without losing their place. In figure 6.2, if you were interested only in the data on the right side of the graph, you could use a zoom feature to focus on that and enlarge the text, making it easier to read. This is a native feature of all but the most basic graph visualization tools; it's included by default with both KeyLines and Gephi. Both products also include adjusting the zoom level through manipulation of the mouse wheel, which is an intuitive navigation method.

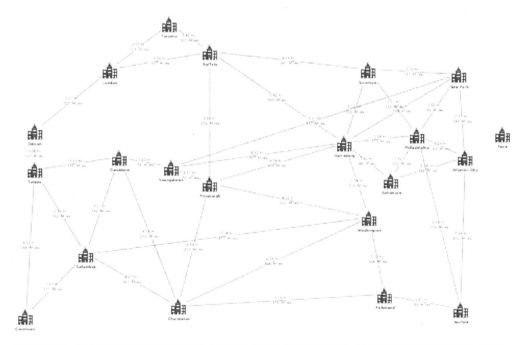

Figure 6.2   **A zoomed-out view showing an entire graph of the distance between North American cities**

Although this chapter has a later section about graphs on mobile platforms, it's worth pointing out that multitouch is becoming an expected interface for mobile applications, where users can drag a finger on the background of the chart to pan around the chart as if they were moving a piece of paper positioned inside the phone or tablet's screen. Or they can pinch their fingers to zoom out or spread their fingertips apart to zoom in on a targeted area, like in figure 6.3.

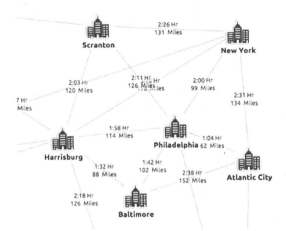

Figure 6.3   Zoomed-in view of a portion of the chart to see more detail

Both KeyLines and Gephi also contain an overview window, also common in image-editing software, that allows a zoomed-in user to see the full chart with a box indicating the area in which they're viewing the detail, as shown in figure 6.4.

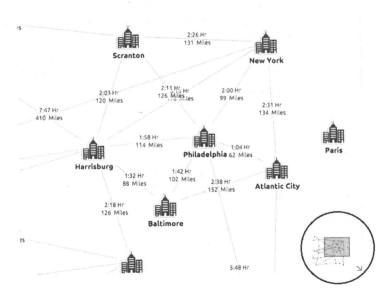

Figure 6.4   Overview window showing the user which subsection of the chart they're viewing

How could enabling zooming and panning help the Abramoff chart? In a newspaper, the amount of data you present on a page is limited by the size of the page. The chart was designed to show the intersection of the two major political bribery scandals in the United States from 2005 and how Brent Wilkes was involved in both, but it barely touches on the Abramoff scandal, the investigation of which, at its peak, had 100 FBI agents dedicated exclusively to uncovering the scope of the corruption. It would be impossible to show all his bribes, clients, and victims on a single page, but in an application where the user could zoom into their area of interest, it would be a fascinating chart.

6.2   *Declutter your charts*

The temptation with graph visualizations is to find some way to put every bit of data you have somewhere on the chart. This will backfire and create a cluttered, ugly chart that's hard to interpret, as demonstrated in figure 6.5.

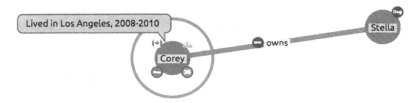

Figure 6.5   This chart is too busy. It's trying to show too many properties on the chart at once.

In figure 6.5, I've used too many visual cues. Multiple glyphs with text, node sizes and colors, node and edge labels, and edge colors make the user's eyes water. This is too much for a user to understand, and most of the data represented this way doesn't need to be presented all at once. It's better to divide properties into two groups: the properties that a user needs to see on the chart initially so that they can determine which nodes or links interest them, and the properties that are interesting to a user after a node has been selected.

When to show properties

What properties should be visible on the chart versus elsewhere?

- Properties visible on the chart should be ones that the user needs to see in order to determine what to focus on.
- Properties that are useful once a user has selected a node can be put external to the visualization elsewhere on the screen.

Which properties fit into which groups will obviously vary based on the use case. In the Abramoff chart, the user doesn't need to see all the text on the links right away. We want to present the user with the connections among the lobbyists, members of Congress, and other companies, but the detail on those connections can be saved for later. That's why in the KeyLines example in figure 6.6 I removed the textual labels from the links.

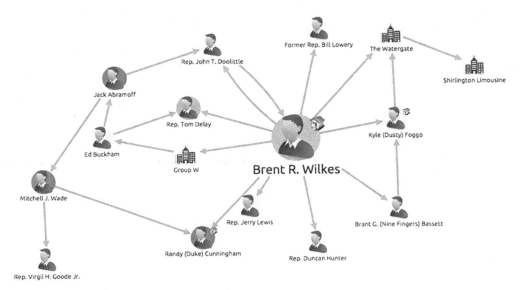

Figure 6.6   A representation of the Abramoff chart with extraneous information on the links removed

So how do we display those properties on individual nodes that we know the user will find useful? Both Gephi and KeyLines have the concept of node or link *selection*, which (just like in text editors) is often done via a mouse click or by dragging a marquee box around multiple chart items. The user action of selecting a node or link is the cue that they want to know more about the item in question, and at that point, it's helpful to display additional detail that would otherwise clutter the chart. There are two common methods to show the user this additional data. One is to show a table outside the visualization with this data when a node or link is selected, as shown in figure 6.7.

The second method would be to overlay a tooltip on top of the chart when the user hovers a mouse over a node or a link. The benefit of this approach is that the user doesn't have to move their eyes from the item they've just selected, but the drawback is that as they move the mouse pointer around, they'll see tooltips and pop-ups constantly appearing and disappearing. See figure 6.8 for an example.

The choice is a matter of taste. Personally, I don't like the busyness that pop-ups create, but others might not mind that. I'd rather reserve some space off the chart surface for this data, especially because it often tends to be narrative and therefore lengthy.

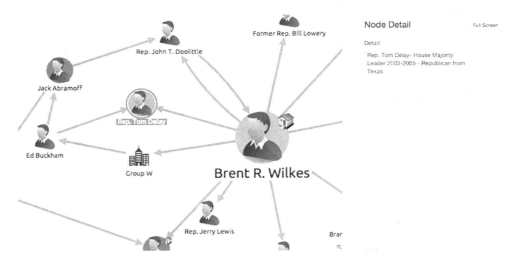

Figure 6.7   A table removed from the visualization displaying additional properties of the selected item

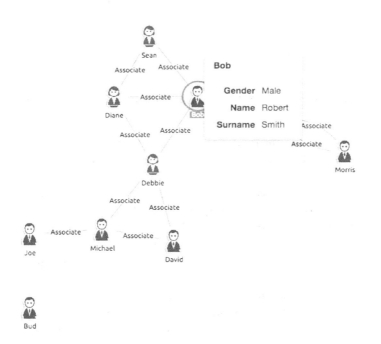

Figure 6.8   A tooltip showing detail of the selected node right on the chart

Gephi doesn't offer the pop-up capability, but I'll show how you can display additional properties in a separate pane in the following section. You'll learn how to code additional properties and pop-ups using KeyLines in section 6.2.2.

6.2.1 *Implementation in Gephi*

Gephi has limited ability to customize the user interface, but there is a way to see the details of the data behind each node (but not links). In the overview window, the left side of the pane offers a number of different modes, which means actions that can be taken upon clicking a node. The very bottom one is titled Edit – Edit Node Attributes. After you select this mode, the upper-left pane will display all known properties of that node in a table. See the screenshot in figure 6.9 for an example.

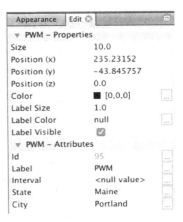

Hovering over a node in Gephi will gray out the rest of the chart except what's directly connected to the focus node. This behavior can't be changed but is often helpful because it allows the user to see which nodes are connected without having to trace through many overlapping lines, as you can see in figure 6.10.

Figure 6.9   The Edit pane in Gephi showing additional property details of a selected node

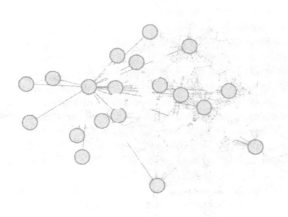

Figure 6.10   Hovering over a node in Gephi will gray out all but the directly connected nodes.

6.2.2   *Implementation in KeyLines*

KeyLines offers a bit more flexibility to customize the user interface but requires Java-Script knowledge. KeyLines has user-driven chart events, which are actions like click, right-click, and hover. Each of those actions can be bound to a JavaScript function using the `chart.bind()` function, but after that, what happens is up to you and your web development expertise—KeyLines doesn't have the native capability for a tabular view or tooltip. We'll add a tooltip to the Abramoff chart with the following code:

```
chart.bind('hover', nodeTooltip);
```

This line tells KeyLines to run the `nodeTooltip` function whenever the mouse hovers over the chart. The details of the `nodeTooltip` function are shown here:

```
function nodeTooltip(id) {
if (id) {

var item = chart.getItem(id);
var coordinates = chart.viewCoordinates(item.x, item.y);
var x = coordinates.x;
var y = coordinates.y;

if (item.type === 'node') {
```

KeyLines will return null if the mouse isn't over a node or link.

We only show the tooltip on nodes here.

Create the HTML code that will fill the tooltip:

```
var html = Mustache.to_html($('#tt_html').html(), {
label: item.t,
party: party,
termStart: item.d.termStart,
termEnd: item.d.termEnd
});
$('#tooltip-container').html(html);

var tooltip = $('#tooltip');

var top = y - (tooltip.height() / 2);

tooltip.css('left', x).css('top', top);
showTooltip();

} else {
closeTooltip();
}

} else {
closeTooltip();
}
        }
```

Add it to the DOM.

Mustache here just formats our HTML tooltip.

.t is the KeyLines property name for the text of the label.

.d is a special property for KeyLines called data; it allows you to store any key/values alongside nodes or links for further reference. Here, we draw the termstart and termend properties from the data on the node.

These functions are omitted from this for clarity. They are in the downloadable source.

A global setting determines how long in milliseconds the mouse must remain still before firing the hover event:

```
chart.options({hover: 500});
```

This results in the tooltip appearing when hovering over nodes after half a second, as shown in figure 6.11. I've chosen to display the congressperson's name, party, and term start and end dates on the tooltip, but you can customize this with any data that you think is relevant, including images or other multimedia.

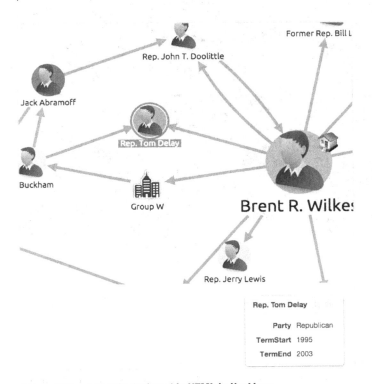

Figure 6.11   A tooltip designed in HTML in KeyLines

So now I've walked you through a few of your options in using chart navigation and interactivity to improve the functionality of your graph. By simplifying what's displayed on the screen, you can wait for the user to ask to see additional information before you show it. Less visual clutter makes for an improved user experience.

6.3   Data volumes

Although good chart navigation can help users better understand a complex, cluttered chart with lots of nodes and links, a far better approach is to avoid presenting complex, cluttered charts to begin with. This is a common mistake with novice graph visualizers, who often want to throw their entire data set on the screen and see if any patterns emerge. More often than not, the result looks like the one in figure 6.12.

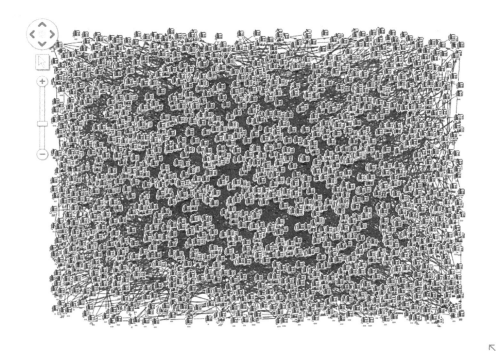

Figure 6.12 An unorganized chart with 2000 nodes

This isn't even a large chart. I routinely get requests to produce charts with tens or even hundreds of thousands of nodes and links. Sometimes extremely large charts do produce some insight. For example, you can see in the graph in figure 6.13 which are the key central nodes holding this structure together, but this is a rare occurrence. More often, the nodes are unclustered and end up looking like the one in figure 6.12. I'll take you through the different approaches to help you represent large sets in tidy, usable graph visualizations.

6.3.1   *Expanding nodes to add data*

If you're not going to draw all the nodes at once, how do you decide which pieces of a larger graph are the relevant ones that your user wants to see? The simple answer is to let your users determine this themselves. A very powerful strategy for graph visualization is to draw query results, not databases. You want your users to indicate what they

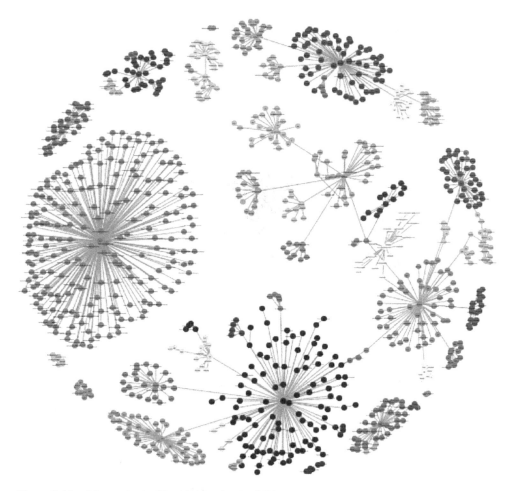

Figure 6.13 A large chart with patterns clearly visible

want to see with a search, visual query, or even a structured query language like SQL or Cypher. This tells you what information they're most interested in, and then you can present those results as a graph. This is a straightforward approach if the data is already in a graph database, because the query languages make it easy for a user to structure a query to say "Show me all the members of Congress who received donations from Brent Wilkes," resulting in a graph similar to the one in figure 6.14.

So instead of plotting the entire US Congress in a graph, which would be too cluttered to make sense of, the user can ask specific questions and see the graph that represents those answers. The user can then *expand* on that graph. Expanding is a method of adding new data to the chart based on user interaction. It's difficult to show complex user interactions in a static book, but the screenshots in figures 6.14, 6.15, and 6.16

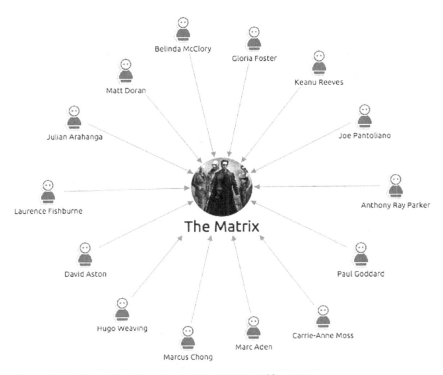

Figure 6.14   The initial view showing *The Matrix* and its actors

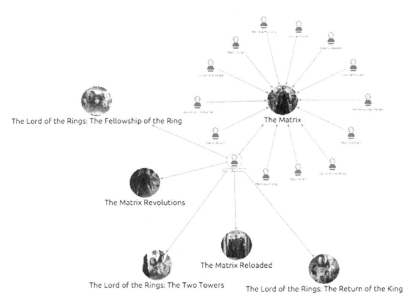

Figure 6.15   Double-clicking Hugo Weaving gives you the movies that he has acted in.

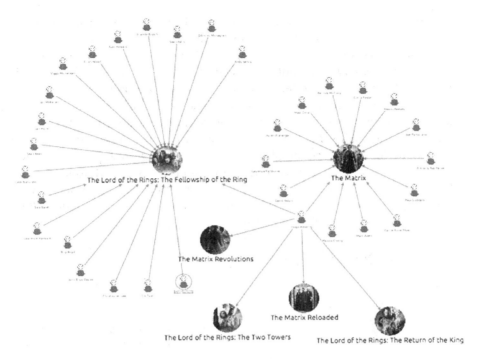

Figure 6.16　Double-clicking *Lord of the Rings* adds the actors in that movie,

should give you some sense of what's going on. Figure 6.14 shows the initial view of an IMDB-type data set with actors and movies.

By double-clicking Hugo Weaving, you can see all the movies he has acted in, as shown in figure 6.15.

Likewise, by double-clicking *Lord of the Rings*, you can see the actors in that movie, as shown in figure 6.16.

In these examples, I have an IMDB (Internet Movie Database) data set with movies and actors. Obviously, plotting all the IMDB data on the screen at the same time isn't feasible, so instead I allow the user to decide where to start. In this case, the user has asked for the first *Matrix* movie and the actors and actresses in that. (I've included only the principal actors for clarity.) As a result of seeing that data, perhaps the user is more interested in Hugo Weaving and wants to *expand* on him, issuing a new query to my data source asking for all the movies that he has been in and returning those to the chart.

DEFINITION　*Expanding* means adding new graph data to a visualization linked to an item already present as a result of a user interaction. This is most often a double-click with the mouse but could be some other user action. When using a graph database, you'll find this to be an easy query to write.

The items that are returned can be customized. With a very dense data set, returning everything connected to a node might result in too much data, so perhaps it should return only links containing a certain property. With a sparse data set, you may want to return the nodes and edges not just one level removed from the selected node but two levels. In the movies example, this would be all the actors in the selected movie *and* the movies in which they have starred. Trial and error is necessary to find the right balance, but I suggest that the typical expand option should return somewhere between 2 and 12 nodes. With more than 12, the chart gets too cluttered to read, and fewer than 2 ends up being less helpful to the user. Also, if an expand operation returns zero nodes, meaning that everything connected to the selected node is already on the chart, you should notify the user of that fact. Otherwise, it's unclear whether the expand operation ran, is still running, or has returned empty. Something like the pop-up shown in figure 6.17 should be sufficient.

Figure 6.17   Dialog box notfiying the user that no new data was added to the chart

Although we'll discuss layouts in more detail in chapter 7, it's important not to run a new layout every time the user expands. This will cause the user to lose their place, and it won't be clear what was on the chart previously versus what was added as a result of the expand operation.

Let's build an expand capability into our Abramoff chart in KeyLines. It makes sense only when there's some sort of data store behind the graph, which isn't really true with the Abramoff chart—I'll leave the database connection part empty in the code because there are so many different ways of connecting JavaScript to a server-side database.

1   We start by binding the double-click event in KeyLines to the JavaScript function we want to run, in this case expandClickedNode:

```
chart.bind('dblclick', expandClickedData);
```

2   Now we have to write what happens in that function:

```
function expandClickedData(clickedID, x, y) {
    if (clickedID) {
      var clickedItem = chart.getItem(clickedID);
      var expandQuery = 'SELECT EVERYTHING LINKED TO NODE ' + clickedID;
```

clickedID is filled in only if the user has clicked a node or a link; otherwise it's empty.

Not a real query

```
callDatabase(expandQuery, function (json){
    var items = makeKeyLinesItems(json);
    chart.expand(items, {fit: true});
});
    }
}
```

Database calls are typically asynchronous, so we write a callback.

The database is unlikely to return data in exactly the right format, so we need to create a function as we did in chapter 4 to translate.

On background click, do nothing

chart.expand merges the new data to the chart.

In KeyLines, the expand function is automatically animated.

6.4   *Animations and mobile*

There are a few other ways that interactions can be enhanced on visualization, including animations and providing touch support for mobile touch devices. We'll go through those in this section.

6.4.1   *Animating charts*

Animations are one of the most exciting ways digital graphs are superior to static graphs. The human brain is able to notice motion much more easily than static images. But moving items around on the screen when it's not in response to user input can be distracting and annoying to a user. Many times a user wants to move a specific node to a specific location, perhaps to make the chart more readable. Although virtually every tool supports this drag-and-drop behavior, many insist on running an additional animated layout after every user action, which is the opposite of what the user is expecting. I strongly suggest turning this auto-animation off if possible.

But animating a layout when prompted by a user action can be really helpful. Because a layout algorithm is complex and can take some time to run, the temptation is to immediately place the chart in the new, laid-out state without showing the user where things are moving. On the contrary, this is an opportunity to use a good animation; it's very easy to lose one's place when the nodes jump from one location to another without showing the transition.

Also helpful is animating visual property changes. If you're going to change the width of a link or the size of a node, the user will pick up those changes more easily if they're animated.

Animating an expand operation is also useful because you can show the nodes exploding out from the selected node to more intuitively demonstrate that new data being added is linked to the selected node.

If user interactions are difficult to describe in a static book, animations are even more difficult. See the animation section on the book's web page for some examples of animations used correctly.

Gephi doesn't permit custom animations, but KeyLines does. The JavaScript code for performing animations in KeyLines is this:

```
chart.animateProperties()
```

This function takes an object or array of chart objects (either nodes or links) along with the properties that you wish to animate. Any numeric or color properties can be animated. For example, the following line will change node 7 from its current color to blue and half blended out:

```
chart.animateProperties({id: '7', c: 'rgba(0,0,255,0.5)'});
```

This line will change the width to 10 of multiple links—links 5 and 10:

```
chart.animateProperties([{id: '5', w:10},{id: '10', w:10}]));
```

The layouts in both KeyLines and Gephi are animated by default.

Many dismiss animations as simply eye candy, but used sparingly and in the right places, they can provide real value.

6.4.2   *Designing for mobile touch environments*

More and more web applications are being built with mobile platforms in mind, and it's only recently that the screen size and resolution of tablets and phones have been sufficient for doing data visualization, even though it's still not quite the same experience as working from a laptop or desktop. But when designing a graph visualization application, it's important to keep the increasing number of mobile users in mind, and designing a mobile UI where the user is unlikely to be using a mouse presents unique challenges.

First, you need to consider what platform (Android versus iOS, for example) your audience is using. Node-link visualizations are complex diagrams that show a lot of detail and require a decent amount of screen space.

As a test, I loaded large charts on my old iPhone 5, but I don't recommend using a phone for any serious application. It's impossible to view any detail, and the user would end up spending more time zooming and panning than they would understanding the data. But tablets are a different story. In addition to the UI challenges, graph visualization applications are unlikely to be self-contained on a mobile device. You'll likely need to store the data on the server side somewhere and allow the tablets and phones to query the data, which—because you're transmitting data over the internet—means you'll need to have a plan for security and user management as well. Those topics are more generic to mobile app development and beyond the scope of this book; I'll focus on what makes the UI on mobile platforms unique for graph visualization. iPads still occupy the majority of the tablet market, though Android tablets are rapidly gaining popularity. You'll likely need to support both.

Second, when designing graph visualizations for tablets, you want to allocate as much space to the visualization as possible. Earlier in the chapter, I recommended allocating screen space outside the visualization to show additional properties of the chart items to the user. Although this may be the best approach for users with large monitors, on a tablet it's likely to just get in the way. For mobile platforms, important data should be available on the surface of the chart itself, not buried behind menu navigations or sidebars.

The third thing to consider is that the user will likely be interacting with the visualization via their fingers, and fingers cover a lot of screen area. So with tightly packed UI elements, like a busy chart with lots of nodes, it's not realistic to expect users to tap individual nodes to perform an action like expanding, unless the nodes are roughly fingertip-size or larger. To avoid this problem, keep the charts smaller, with fewer items than you would use on an application for a larger screen. Additionally, people use more than one finger on their phones, so *multitouch gestures* (interaction with more than one fingertip at a time) are generally expected. As mentioned earlier in this chapter, users familiar with touch devices will want to pinch their fingers to zoom in and spread them apart to zoom out. Even more-complex multitouch gestures using three, four, or even five fingers might be helpful in certain circumstances.

Graph visualization on mobile platforms is a new area, and the existing tools haven't caught up yet. Gephi is Windows-only software, so although it may work on the Microsoft Surface, it won't work on iOS or Android devices. KeyLines is supported on iOS, Android, and Microsoft touch devices with some basic touch events, but only in the browser, not as a native app. Right now, there doesn't seem to be a native mobile graph app available, which means there might be an opportunity for an enterprising graph developer to create one.

6.5 *Summary*

In this chapter, you learned the following:

- Navigation is an important feature for all but the most trivial graph visualizations, and this feature is native in most visualization applications and toolkits.
- Some properties are important to include on the surface of the chart—those things that help the user decide which nodes to focus on—but others should be saved for after the user has selected a node or link.
- Tooltips are helpful for reducing clutter. Neither KeyLines nor Gephi includes them by default, but they can be added in KeyLines with a few dozen lines of code.
- When you have too much data to present at once, allowing the user to expand as they explore the data can be very valuable.
- Animations are helpful, but use them too much and you risk losing your user's attention.
- Support for mobile platforms is important, but designing for a touch interface is also important because it's different from a mouse interface.

How to organize a chart

This chapter covers

- Layouts and why they're important
- The force-directed layout variants and when they're helpful
- Other useful layouts for specific data structures
- The drawbacks of 3D rendering

Unlike many other data visualizations, in a graph visualization the actual location of nodes on the screen has no inherent meaning. Nothing is different about a node that's located at the upper-left corner of the screen versus one at the bottom right. This is in stark contrast to something like an XY scatter plot where the location of the item on a Cartesian plane tells you the value of specific properties of that item. In node-link-style graph visualizations, the location of the node is determined by convenience and readability. Nodes should be placed in locations that make the chart less cluttered and easier to read. Unfortunately, automated layout algorithms aren't magic. Once the number of nodes and edges on a chart gets into the hundreds, no layout will manage to make it readable. One of the most common requests I get with larger charts is to detangle the links, or prevent links from crossing one another. With most charts, this isn't possible because of the limitations of 2D geometry.

There have been decades of academic research into the domain of graph drawing, which is a mathematical subfield consumed with determining algorithmically the best way to organize a chart for readability. In this chapter, we'll discuss some of the most common layout algorithms, how they work, and when they're useful.

Automated layouts are often only the first step, helping to get the chart into a semi-coherent state. As mentioned in chapter 6, you'll definitely want to allow for a measure of manual layout, which is simply dragging the nodes around by hand to create a pleasing layout. Table 7.1 lists the layouts we'll discuss in this chapter and when they can be valuable.

Table 7.1   Popular layouts and when they're most helpful

Layout name	Typical example	Detail	Thumbnail
Force-directed layout (ForceAtlas, Fruchterman-Reingold, and many others)	TCP/IP computer networks, social network analysis	▪ Provides a decent result regardless of the structure of the data ▪ Tends to put the best-connected nodes near the center ▪ Creates starburst effect around nodes with lots of links ▪ Can be slow to compute	
Circular layout	Token ring computer network	▪ Can work well for sparse graphs ▪ Nodes can be organized by some property value (largest to smallest, for example) ▪ Fast to compute ▪ Ugly for dense graphs	
Hierarchical layout	Corporate reporting structure	▪ Great if your data has a rigid tree structure ▪ Terrible otherwise	
Radial layout	Most-wanted poster	▪ Helpful for focusing on specific nodes and inspecting distance (number of links) from that nod ▪ Quick to compute	

Table 7.1   Popular layouts and when they're most helpful (continued)

Layout name	Typical example	Detail	Thumbnail
Structural layout	IMDb	<ul><li>Puts nodes in groups based on similar structure</li><li>Structure means the nodes are linked to the same things</li><li>Helpful when trying to identify similar nodes based on linkages</li><li>Ugly for dense, large graphs</li></ul>	
3D layout	Very few	<ul><li>Looks really cool</li><li>Has very little practical value</li></ul>	

With large numbers of nodes and links, it would be too time-consuming to manually place them on a page where they should all go. Layouts use algorithms to determine the position of nodes, so it's important to select the right one for the type of data you have. In this chapter, we'll review the layout options in more detail: when they can clarify the data in a graph and when they just create more confusion.

7.1   *Force-directed layouts*

Force-directed layout algorithms are the most common method of graph drawing because they're mathematically simple to write and can create decent results across different graph data structures. It's also a good place to start if you don't know the data well enough to know whether a different layout might be more useful. This layout is common enough that graph visualizations are occasionally called force diagrams. The basic tenet behind force-directed layouts is that the graph is modeled like a physical system, and the model is run to determine where nodes end up.

In this model, each pair of nodes has either an attractive force or a repulsive force, depending on whether there's an edge between them. This means that two nodes that have a link between them want to be closer together—imagine a spring between them or a gravitational force, as in figure 7.1.

Nodes that don't have an edge between them are repulsed from one another, as shown in figure 7.2.

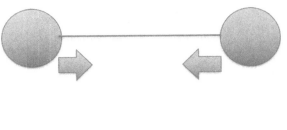

Figure 7.1 Nodes that have an edge between them are attracted to one another.

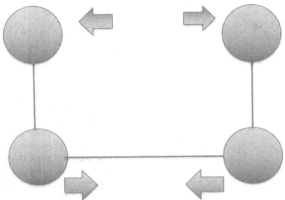

Figure 7.2 Nodes that don't have an edge between them are repulsed from one another.

If linked nodes were attracted to one another without limit, the endpoint of the algorithm would result in them all stacked on top of each other, so another feature of this layout is that there's an ideal link length. The attractive force is attractive only when the nodes are farther apart than that length, and it's otherwise repulsive.

After the calculation is run, each node has a force vector associated with it, being pushed away from nodes that it's not connected to and toward (mostly) nodes that it is. The algorithm then moves each node a small bit in that direction and the result is run again, typically until the result stabilizes (for some implementations) or for a fixed number of iterations (for many other implementations). Figure 7.3 shows the force-directed result on a medium-size graph.

Force-directed algorithms are *nondeterministic*, meaning that the layout algorithm won't automatically create the same chart from the same graph each time. It varies significantly based on the starting position of the nodes, which is random in most force-directed algorithms because there's no a priori criterion to place the nodes. This is a drawback of the layout because two people running the same layout on the same chart data could get dramatically different results, to the point that they don't even look similar. Figure 7.4 shows two examples of the same force-directed layout creating two different charts because the starting positions of the nodes were different.

The basic force-directed layout can be customized by tweaking the power of the attractive and repulsive forces, and it will produce different results. A high attractive

Figure 7.3   The force-directed layout spreads unconnected nodes apart, allowing you to see the graph structure. The algorithm has run enough times that this is the stabilized result, where none of the nodes have large forces against them.

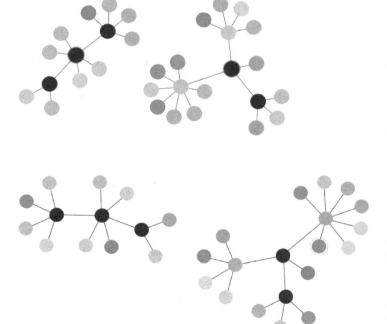

Figure 7.4   The top chart and the bottom chart are force-directed layouts of the same chart data but appear different because of the random starting position of the nodes when the layout is run.

force will result in a tightly packed chart with short links, whereas a high repulsive force will result in a spread-out chart with longer links. In Gephi, this can be customized on the Layout pane of the application. In KeyLines, both variables are packed into a single parameter called *tightness*, which controls the ratio of the attractive versus repulsive forces. Figures 7.5 and 7.6 show an example of a tight chart versus a spread-out one.

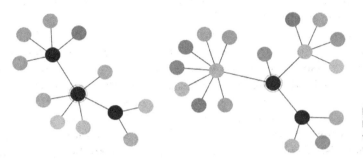

Figure 7.5   A layout with a high attractive force makes for short links and a dense visualization.

Figure 7.5 shows a layout that conserves space but doesn't leave a lot of room for detailed annotations. Figure 7.6 takes up more space, but with thinner links and smaller nodes, it leaves more white space where you could show more detail.

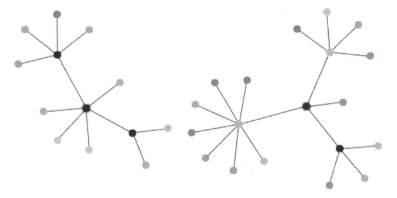

Figure 7.6   A layout with a low attractive force results in a spread-out look.

Although the force-directed class of layouts is good in that it works well across many different structures of graphs, there are two drawbacks, namely, the speed of execution and stacking of nodes.

DRAWBACKS
The vanilla force-directed layout can be quite slow. The number of calculations is typically scaled with the square of the number of nodes (each node has to be compared to every other node in order to calculate the force, and this must be recalculated for

each iteration), which can very quickly become unwieldy. Some more-modern algorithms can scale better, to O(N*log(N)). Even on faster hardware, large charts with tens of thousands of nodes can take minutes to compute. In view of this, some layout algorithms take shortcuts. Because the value of the force vector varies with the square of the distance between the nodes, faraway nodes often have a negligible contribution and can be ignored. This can significantly speed up the algorithm because it needs to calculate only the force from linked nodes and nearby unlinked nodes, with almost no impact on the quality of the result.

Another drawback of force-directed algorithms is that they don't typically respect the boundaries of other nodes, meaning that they will likely allow nodes to overlap one another. In some cases, this can be beneficial, because if you're concerned only with showing the overall structure of the data and not the details of each node, allowing them to overlap can save space. But more often you want the entirety of each node to be visible. This adds to the complexity of the layout, because now it must also calculate whether the extent of each node overlaps another (and remember that many good visualizations have different-size nodes, so those extents are different for each one). A common workaround is, instead of calculating these overlaps after each iteration, to calculate them at the end and then slightly shuffle the nodes so that each is visible. Figure 7.7 shows a graph layout where nodes are allowed to overlap.

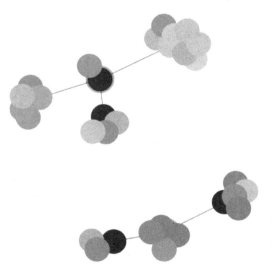

Figure 7.7   A force-directed algorithm that allows nodes to overlap saves space but comes at the expense of seeing the details of each item.

7.1.1   Force-directed layouts in Gephi

Now let's see these layouts in action. First, let's look at Gephi, which offers a number of force-directed layouts. These options are available on the Layout pane at the lower left of the main visualization. You can see the Layout pane with some options in figure 7.8.

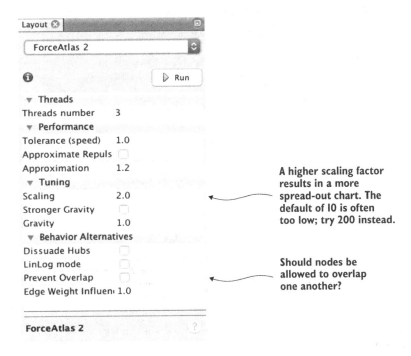

Figure 7.8   The Layout pane of Gephi. Most layouts run continuously until you tell them to stop.

Although additional layouts can be added using the plugin capability, we'll concentrate on the two main force-directed layouts included with the base Gephi package: ForceAtlas and Fruchterman-Reingold.

ForceAtlas is the most common force-directed layout we've discussed, and Gephi lets you tweak the attractive versus repulsive force via parameters set on the Layout pane. Figure 7.9 shows our Abramoff chart in Gephi with the default Force-Atlas layout applied. (I suggest opening Gephi while reading along so that you can see the animations.) In figure 7.8, I used the ForceAtlas2 layout but had to make a modification. The default parameters allowed too tight a cluster, so this diagram reflects a scaling factor of 200 as opposed to 10. This is the ratio of the repulsive force to the attractive one, so the higher the number, the more spread out the chart will be.

Note that our subject, Brent R. Wilkes, was put at the center of the chart automatically. Because the nodes connect to him but not to each other, they create a starburst

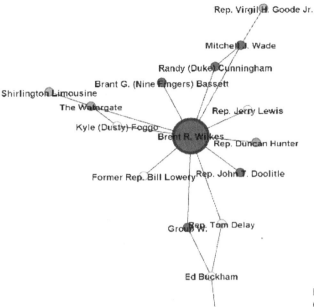

Figure 7.9   The ForceAtlas layout in Gephi puts our subject, Brent Wilkes, near the center of the chart.

effect around him. This is a common effect of nearly all the force-directed layouts and can be helpful for identifying the best-connected nodes in the chart.

Now let's look at the Fruchterman-Reingold layout using the same chart data. Although both are force-directed layouts, there's a noticeable difference in how the chart looks. Without going into painful mathematical detail (which you can view here, if you're interested: http://mng.bz/L9GX), Fruchterman-Reingold tends to uniformly distribute the nodes across the surface of the chart. It's an older layout with fewer options to tweak, which technically makes it inferior to the ForceAtlas layouts, but fewer options means that there are fewer ways to break the layout by setting bad properties. Thus, you're more likely to get a more aesthetically pleasing visualization. This is usually my first choice when working in Gephi. Figure 7.10 shows the same Abramoff chart run with the Fruchterman-Reingold layout algorithm.

Because Gephi runs the layouts continuously, you can play with the parameters in the Layout pane to get the result you want. Simply run the layout and leave it running. Then you can change parameters (like scaling, gravity, and overlapping) and see the result immediately reflected on the chart.

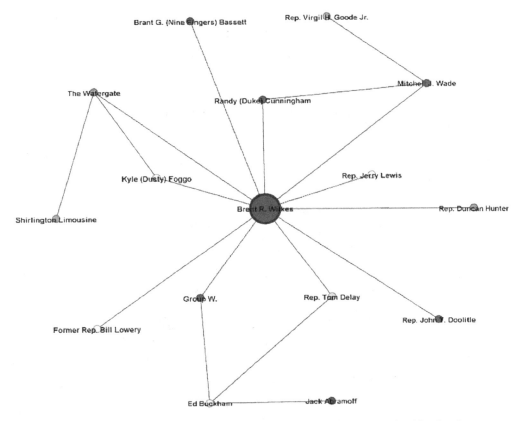

Figure 7.10 The same Abramoff chart when the Fruchterman-Reingold layout algorithm has been run

7.1.2 *Implementation in KeyLines*

It's up to you to decide how much layout flexibility to expose to your users as part of your application. KeyLines has only one force-directed layout, which they call the Standard layout, and only one parameter of that layout, called *tightness*. The typical scenario in a visualization application is to provide the UI for users to run layouts on demand, typically with buttons. So that's what we'll do with the Abramoff app that we're building in KeyLines. We'll add the following line to our HTML to create a button for the Standard layout:

```
<input type="button" value="Standard" id="standardlayout">
```

Next, we need to tell the application what to do when the user clicks the button. This is in the JavaScript. (The $ notation is the use of jQuery, which is optional but helpful.)

```
$('#standardlayout').click(applyStandardLayout);
```

This line tells the app to run the `applyStandardLayout` function when the button is clicked, so we also need to write that function:

```
function applyStandardLayout() {
  chart.layout('standard');
}
```

Now, when the user clicks the button labeled Standard on the web page, the Standard layout will run, and the result will look something like figure 7.11.

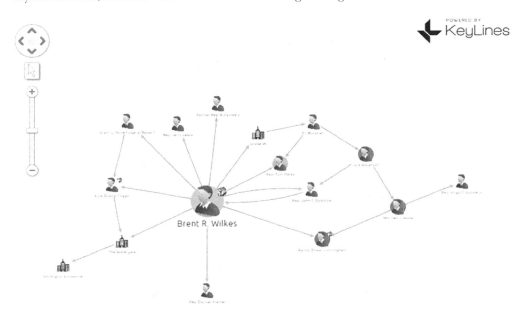

Figure 7.11   The Standard layout applied to the Abramoff chart in KeyLines

There are a number of parameters on the layout function call, the key ones being whether the result is animated, whether the nodes should allow for overlap (tidy), and the tightness of the result. In the following code snippet, we apply a little more control over how the result looks. The tightness property ranges from 0 to 10, with 5 as the default, so we choose a slightly looser layout than the default:

```
chart.layout('standard', {tightness: 4, animate: true, tidy: true});
```

7.2   *Other layout options*

Although force-directed layouts are the most popular, other layout algorithms may be useful with certain structures for your data. As I referenced at the beginning of the chapter, different charts are best used in different circumstances. If you have a sparse graph, with each node having only one or two links, the circular layout will let you see patterns in that data easily. But with denser charts, the circular layout becomes very messy because the links all cross each other. Hierarchical layouts can be helpful if your data has a tree structure to it, meaning nodes are linked to nodes only at adjacent levels, but they're not helpful otherwise. Radial layouts put a node or a group of nodes in the center of the chart and organize everything else around it, so they can be helpful if you have one specific focus on the chart and need to see how everything else relates to the focus node. KeyLines has a unique layout called the Structural layout, which creates circular clusters of nodes that all are linked to the same other nodes and runs a force-directed layout treating those clusters themselves as nodes. It's an interesting approach that can be helpful in specific circumstances but can also look terrible.

7.2.1 Circular layouts

The circular layout involves taking all the charts, organizing them in a big circle, and drawing the links as straight lines between them. Figure 7.12 shows an example from a computer network where the circular layout is a helpful orientation. Most connections are internal to each colored subdomain, but the large number of connections from green nodes to purple ones is immediately visible, which could be by design, or it could be worthy of taking a closer look.

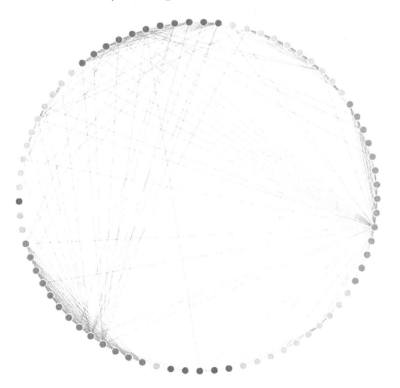

Figure 7.12   A useful implementation of the circular layout

In this example, you can see helpful patterns in the organization. One orange node is the best connected to other groups throughout the network, most of the purple nodes connect to other purple nodes, and fewer links go all the way across the chart. Another feature of the circular layout is that it doesn't bias any particular node by putting it toward the center. If you want to avoid drawing the user's eye toward specific nodes, the circular layout, by treating nodes equally, is one of the best options. In spite of this example, however, I rarely find circles to be useful ways of organizing graphs. Often your data will end up looking like figure 7.13.

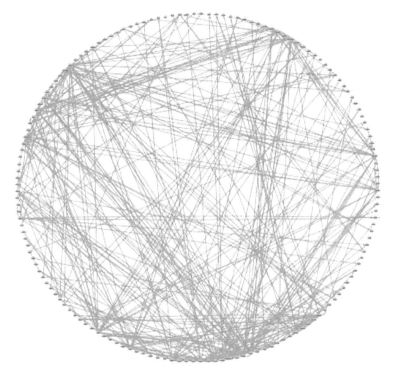

Figure 7.13   A terrible instance of the circular layout

This is the Enron chart from chapter 1 arranged with a circular layout. Because it's a dense chart, with a high number of connections, there's no easy way to make sense of any patterns in the data, and zooming in closely enough to see the details of the nodes means that you can no longer determine the endpoint of any particular link.

IMPLEMENTATION

Gephi doesn't have a circular layout by default, but you can add one as a plugin from the Gephi marketplace here: https://marketplace.gephi.org/plugin/circular-layout/.

After you install this plugin, the circular layout with some interesting parameters will appear in the Layout pane of the Gephi UI.

In KeyLines, the circular layout is treated differently from the other layouts—it's called an arrangement and can be accessed with the `chart.arrange` function. Not that I'd recommend it, but let's add a circular layout button to our Abramoff chart that we've been working on. First, we add another button to the HTML:

```
<input type="button" value="Circle" id="circlelayout">
```

This will add the button to the page; now we'll go into the JavaScript and define what that button does:

```
$('#circlelayout').click(applyCircleLayout);

function applyCircleLayout(evt) {
chart.arrange('circle', chart.selection()});
}
```

This will take the selected nodes (`chart.selection()` is an array of the selected nodes) and arrange them in a circle when the user clicks the button. The result on our chart is shown in figure 7.14.

Figure 7.14   The Abramoff chart, arranged as a circle. It's not a useful layout for this data.

Although a circle isn't the worst layout choice for the Abramoff data, the chart looks cluttered and the links intersect, which can be confusing when zoomed in.

7.2.2   *Hierarchy layout*

If your data is organized as a strict hierarchy, then using a tree to display that can be valuable. But most graph data doesn't have this format. This means that every node can be linked to only one upstream node but can have multiple downstream nodes. A corporate reporting structure is the most common example of a hierarchy, with a single CEO at the top, various levels of management who report toward the CEO in the middle, and workers who report to their managers at the bottom. This is shown in figure 7.15.

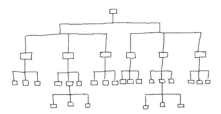

Figure 7.15   A corporate hierarchy with the CEO at the top

A strict hierarchy is also called a directed acyclic graph (DAG). One misplaced link can break the hierarchy, though. If we had one person who reported to two different managers, as shown in figure 7.16, we'd no longer have a strict hierarchy. This is why hierarchical layouts are not versatile. There's no way to define that structure if you have links that break the rules.

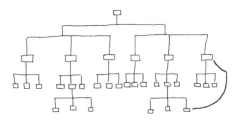

Figure 7.16   A broken hierarchy because one person reports to two managers, causing problems with the hierarchical layout

Corporate structures aren't the only type of data that's organized in hierarchies. A sports tournament bracket is another good example, as is the Windows file structure. (A file sits in a folder, which can sit in another folder, up to the top level on the drive. Virtual folders or links break this structure, however.) IT infrastructure is another example where I've seen hierarchies. In figure 7.17, I show a server, the hosts on that server, the services that run on those hosts, and the business units that use those services.

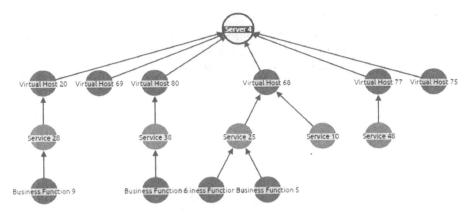

Figure 7.17 A hierarchy as applied to an IT environment

IMPLEMENTATION

Gephi doesn't have a hierarchy layout by default, but a directed acyclic graph layout is available as a plugin. I'm not too impressed with the quality, but it can be helpful as a starting point. You can download it here: https://marketplace.gephi.org/plugin/dag-layout/#.

Like the circular layout, it will then show up in the Layout pane. In Gephi, the apex of the hierarchy, the CEO, will be automatically chosen, and that's based on the direction of the links, so all links have to have downward-pointing arrows in order for the DAG layout to work.

In KeyLines, the hierarchy layout will allow you (or your user) to specify the apex of the hierarchy. KeyLines won't automatically calculate the apex even if you do have arrowheads on your links, though it would be straightforward to do that in your JavaScript by working backwards. As before, we'll add the hierarchy layout option to our Abramoff chart and give the user the ability to select the apex. Add the following to your HTML to put the button on the page:

```
<input type="button" value="Hierarchy" id="hierarchylayout">
```

And bind it to the KeyLines hierarchy layout with the following JavaScript:

```
$('#hierarchylayout').click(applyHierarchyLayout);

function applyHierarchyLayout(evt) {

if(checkSelection('#hierarchylayout')){
chart.layout('hierarchy', {top:chart.selection()});
  }
}
```

An item must be selected to define the apex.

Now, clicking the Hierarchy button with Brent R. Wilkes selected shows what's in figure 7.18: a decent layout of the data, showing how Brent Wilkes is the key figure in
this conspiracy. It's not a true DAG, though, because the chart shows Ed Buckham
connected to both Tom Delay and Group W, but it's close.

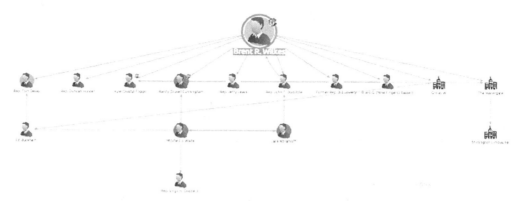

**Figure 7.18   The KeyLines hierarchy layout applied to the Abramoff chart with Brent Wilkes at the
apex. Notice that there are a few rule-breaking links but not enough to destroy the appearance.**

7.2.3   *Radial layout*

Radial layouts are similar to circular layouts with one key difference: bias. Whereas the
circular layout is designed to not highlight any particular node and therefore not bias
the viewer into thinking that any one node is more important than the others, a radial
layout has the exact opposite intention. It takes a node or group of nodes and explicitly puts them in the center and then organizes the rest of the chart around them. If
you know in advance what the key nodes are in the data, this can be a huge improvement over a circular layout. In figure 7.19, I've taken the movies chart from earlier in
the book and run the radial layout around the actress Carrie-Anne Moss. You can see
that everything in the data is within two links of her, so the algorithm has created two
concentric circles around her: one for the movies that she has acted in, and the far circle for the actors and actresses in those movies.

Like the other layouts we've discussed, it's not included by default in Gephi but
available as a plugin on the marketplace here: https://marketplace.gephi.org/plugin/
concentric-layout/. Once installed, it will appear along with the other layouts in the
Layout pane in the UI.

And like the other layouts in KeyLines, it's available with a function call in the API,
using the `top` property to identify the center just like the hierarchy layout. We'll add

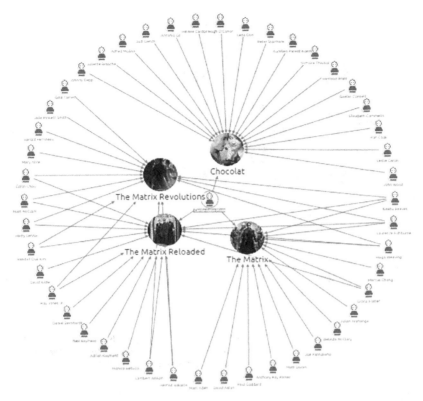

Figure 7.19 The radial layout shows that Carrie-Anne Moss has acted in both the *Matrix* **movies and** *Chocolat.*

this to our Abramoff chart alongside the others with the following changes to the HTML and JavaScript:

```
<input type="button" value="Radial" id="radiallayout">

$('#radiallayout').click(applyRadialLayout);

function applyRadialLayout(evt) {
if(checkSelection('#radiallayout')){
chart.layout('radial', {top:chart.selection()});
 }
}
```

Like the hierarchy layout, this requires a selection.

The KeyLines result on the Abramoff chart is shown in figure 7.20.

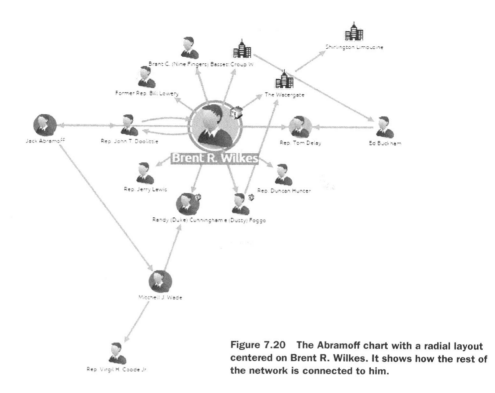

Figure 7.20   The Abramoff chart with a radial layout centered on Brent R. Wilkes. It shows how the rest of the network is connected to him.

7.2.4   *3D layouts*

So far, we've focused on two-dimensional graph visualizations, intended for display on a flat computer monitor. From very early in computer graphics, however, there has been an interest in visualizing graphs in three dimensions. The theory is that issues with complex graphs with crossing edges can be eliminated because nodes can always be placed behind one another, and the camera can be rotated to give the user an intuitive sense of how nodes cluster and which groups are connected to one another. Thus, for a while, images like figure 7.21 were commonplace.

Nowadays 3D visualizations are easy to render using current hardware-accelerated technologies, such as WebGL. Force-directed layouts, because they simply calculate a vector for the movement of each node, are easy to adapt for 3D over 2D. 3D has yet to be embraced by the visualization community and for good reason. Because nodes have to be sized based on their distance from the camera in a 3D visualization, you lose the ability to size nodes according to a property in the data, as we discussed in chapter 5. Also, it's impossible to see the entire graph at once, because some nodes will be occluded behind others.

Another drawback is that links can be very hard to see. There may be a complex structure of links that appear to the eye as a single line if they are all in a plane, similar to the way Saturn's rings show complexity when viewed from one angle but are just a

Figure 7.21 A 3D graph visualization superimposed on a 2D page

line when viewed edge-on. Neither Gephi nor KeyLines nor any of the other tools described in the appendix support 3D graphs. With the advent of virtual-reality goggles that track head movements and 3D gesture control, it's possible that we'll see some more value in 3D as virtual reality becomes more commonplace, but it still seems pretty far off.

7.3   *Summary*

In this chapter, you learned the following:

- A layout is just the visual organization of the data and it doesn't affect the underlying structure.
- Different layouts can be helpful given the structure in your data.
- Force-directed layouts are great for generic data, when you don't otherwise know the structure; they can be helpful for larger charts and are generally quick to execute.
- Radial layouts are helpful to focus on a particular node or nodes by showing how everything else on the chart is connected to it/them.

- Circular layouts aren't that helpful, but they do eliminate bias on charts by placing each node equally distant from the center, and they can be helpful when most connections are within groups and not between them.
- Hierarchy layouts are great when your data follows a strict directed acyclic graph format or is at least close, but they can appear as a jumbled mess otherwise.
- The layouts in Gephi are in the Layout pane, and other layouts can be added via plugins from the marketplace.
- `chart.layout` is the command for running a layout in KeyLines; I showed how to create buttons that call the layouts.
- 3D visualizations and layouts haven't been popular so far, but technology advances might get them some traction in the future.

Big data: using graphs
when there's too much data

This chapter covers

- The limits of graph visualization, both web and desktop
- Abstracting individual data endpoints
- Filtering the chart by type or other metrics
- Grouping nodes and links

In chapter 6, we talked about data volumes and explained how it's not always realistic to draw a chart showing every data endpoint in your data set on the screen at once. This is important to keep in mind when working with large data sets, and some of the techniques we discussed in that chapter, such as allowing the user to navigate the chart, can be useful when working with thousands or even tens of thousands of nodes. One of my company's clients is a credit card–processing company that handles 24,000 transactions every second. There's no way to even think about trying to draw each transaction in a graph visualization. I think the *big data* buzzword gets thrown around needlessly sometimes, but that is truly big data. So should we even bother with graph visualization in those cases? Maybe. We'll start small and work our way up.

In this chapter, I'll talk about some techniques for working with large volumes of data such as filtering and grouping, which can help because they allow your audience to focus only on the bits of the data that are relevant to them. But even when you are fully taking advantage of those techniques, or displaying subsets of the data based on user queries, occasionally the data is so large that a graph may not be the best way to show it. We'll go into that as well.

By the end of this chapter, you'll know how to visualize larger volumes of data, in situations where there's too much data to plot every point. But first, let's explore the best ways to filter data to avoid visual clutter.

8.1 Controlling which nodes and edges are visible

One of the key points of this chapter is that it's not always useful to see all the data at once. Or at least, once you do see all the data, the next step should be deciding how to filter your data to only the bits that are most relevant to your analysis. Figure 8.1 shows a graph that I made from a customer's email data set, similar to the Enron example that we looked at in chapter 1, where each person at the company is a node and the fact that two people emailed one another is a link between them. It's important to note that thousands of records can be represented by a single link—the link itself only shows that two people have communicated; it doesn't reveal whether they communicated once or thousands of times. This design decision alone—linking only if two people ever communicated over email—can reduce the amount drawn significantly, because in this data set, among many others, there are many instances of repeated transactions that only need be drawn once. We can use visual properties of that link to show the number of communications represented by it.

In figure 8.1 you can see every employee of the company in the center of the graph and links to every person each employee has emailed.

On the book's website, there's a colored version of this chart. In that version, I colored the nodes that represent internal employees of the company to show their department: red for sales, yellow for technology, pink for marketing, and so on. Contacts external to the company were left gray. This makes the structure of the graph a little easier to see because the colors stand out from the clutter. Unsurprisingly, the salespeople communicate with most of the external addresses, whereas the admin and marketing people talk mostly among themselves. This is still too much data, however, to make good sense of what's going on in the chart. One of the most basic ways of controlling the amount drawn is to filter the data to view only the information relevant to the task at hand. Because each employee's department is one of the properties that we have on the nodes, let's look at what the chart in figure 8.1 looks like when we filter down to just two departments, as shown in figure 8.2.

In figure 8.2 I've run a filter to hide everyone except for marketing and admin employees. The result is that patterns of communication between the two departments are more visually apparent. For example, the key communication point between the two departments seems to be from Caleb (marketing, in pink) to Harper (admin,

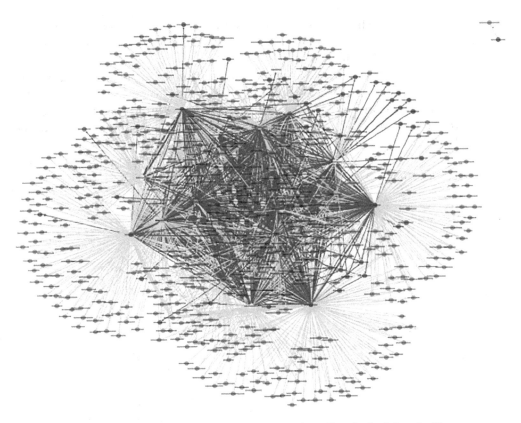

Figure 8.1 An anonymized company's internal and external email contacts. Internal addresses are colored nodes and external addresses are gray.

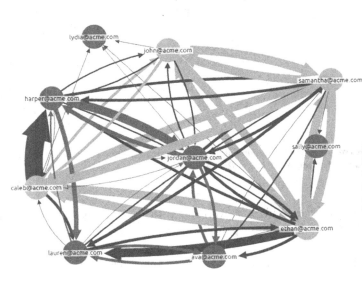

Figure 8.2 The chart from figure 8.1 filtered to show only marketing (pink) and admin (brown) employees and their communications. This allows you to identify some takeaways, like how much more frequently marketing employees email one another.

in brown), which you can see from the width of the link, compared to the other links drawn on the chart. In that case, I was filtering by a property on the node, but it can also be helpful to filter links.

In figure 8.3 you see a network of airline flights. The original data set shows flights from all US airlines, but I've already filtered to show only flights on two different airlines: Alaska Airlines (blue/darker) and JetBlue (brown/lighter). This graph shows that there's very little overlap between the two route systems: Seattle and Portland to New York and Boston are the only routes where both airlines offer service. The lack of overlap may make one airline an attractive acquisition for the other; that's one reason graph visualization can be a very useful tool for companies exploring mergers.

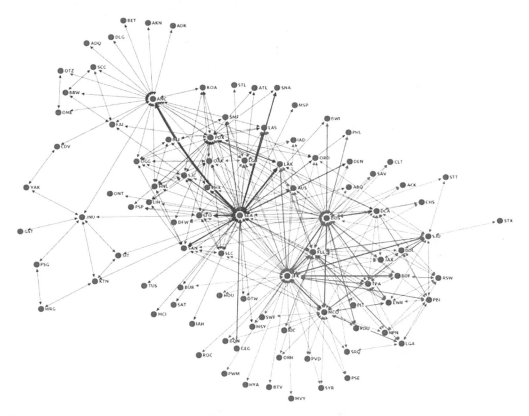

Figure 8.3   The route maps of Alaska Airlines and JetBlue drawn as a graph. Graphing the destination cities makes it apparent that there's little route overlap between the airlines.

But I can take this chart and filter it even more to focus even further on the most important bits. I can filter according to any criteria. Filtering lets you ignore the routes where there aren't many flights and focus on solely the busiest routes, those with more than 2,800 flights per year, or roughly 7 per day. In figure 8.4 I've shown

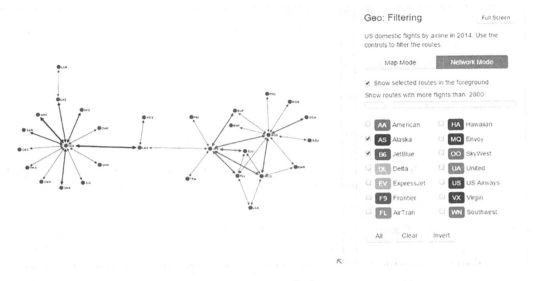

Figure 8.4 The Alaska Airlines and JetBlue routes with more than seven flights per day

the filtering UI so that you can see the various filters I've applied; in this case I've filtered by airline and number of flights on the route. And the result is interesting and useful. We see no overlap between the Alaska Airlines busiest routes and the JetBlue busiest routes. Nearly all the busy routes on JetBlue are from New York JFK or Boston, with only a single exception (Long Beach to Las Vegas).

There are two different methods of filtering: filtering before bringing the data into the visualization and letting the visual tool do the filtering. Both have benefits and drawbacks, as shown in table 8.1.

Table 8.1 The benefits and drawbacks of filtering on the data side versus the visual side

	Benefit	Drawback
Database filtering	No limit to the size of the data set as long as a reasonable amount of data is rendered. Limited only by the creativeness of your queries. Visual performance not affected.	Queries can get very complex and time consuming with multiple filters. Removing or adding a new filter requires a new query to the database. The visual tool doesn't know about the filtered data.
Visual filtering	Everything is done in the tool; doesn't require a persistent connection to the data source. Filtered items are still in memory and can be brought back easily. No need to design complex queries.	Limited by the memory available—extremely large data sets won't work. Filters are limited to computer power on the individual machine; no scaling. Filtering limited to the capabilities of the chosen visual tool.

Filtering on the data side is straightforward. In the airline flights example, if the data were in a relational database, you'd just use the appropriate WHERE statement to get back only the data you want and then insert that data into your visual tool, something like the following:

```
SELECT * FROM route
WHERE NumFlights > 2800
AND (Airline="AS" OR Airline="B6")
```

The problem occurs when the user decides they also want to see Southwest Airlines; you have to go back to the database to get more data, possibly creating server overhead and introducing a lag. Therefore, in some cases, it can make sense to apply filters directly in the visual layer itself. Next, we'll go through how to build filters in both Gephi and KeyLines.

8.1.1   Filtering in Gephi

Gephi has a good user interface for implementing complex filters on the left side of the overview window. I'll show you how to use it by going back to our Abramoff example chart from previous chapters, as shown in figure 8.5.

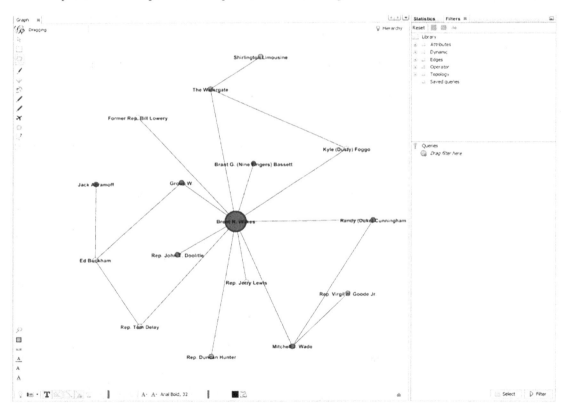

Figure 8.5   The Abramoff chart we built in Gephi starting in chapter 5. The Filters pane is on the right.

Before we can run any helpful filters, we need to add some data that we can filter on, because right now the chart has only the names of the individuals involved. To edit the data within Gephi, we switch to the Data Laboratory panel located in the top center of the window. This will bring up a spreadsheet-type view of the data, as shown in figure 8.6.

Figure 8.6   The data laboratory view of the Abramoff chart

Now we have to give each node and link some properties. Earlier, we used color-coding to indicate whether that person had been indicted or was under investigation, so let's add that data back in. Since we're looking at only a dozen nodes on this chart, we'll just type it right into Gephi. We'll do that by clicking the Add Column button at the bottom of the screen and creating a column titled Indicted with a Boolean data type. Then we'll check the boxes of those who have been indicted (according to the original *New York Times* article). You can follow along with figure 8.7.

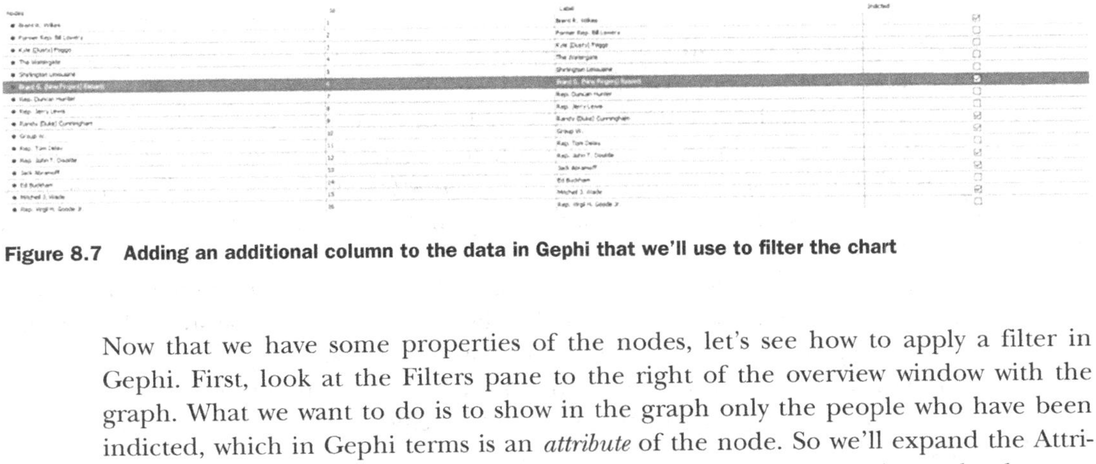

Figure 8.7   Adding an additional column to the data in Gephi that we'll use to filter the chart

Now that we have some properties of the nodes, let's see how to apply a filter in Gephi. First, look at the Filters pane to the right of the overview window with the graph. What we want to do is show in the graph only the people who have been indicted, which in Gephi terms is an *attribute* of the node. So we'll expand the Attributes folder. At the next level down, we want to look at only those items that have an attribute equal to a value, in this case, true, so we'll expand the Equal folder. Then we see a list of all the attributes on nodes in our chart, including the indicted flag that we just created. So let's take that value, Indicted, and drag it to the bottom pane, where we build the filter. See the screen shot in figure 8.8 for guidance.

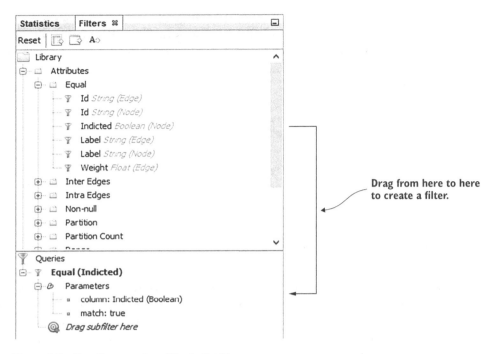

Figure 8.8   Creating a custom filter in Gephi

Because Indicted is a Boolean property, we're asked if we want to match to True or False; clicking True and then Apply Filter filters the Gephi chart to show us only the nodes representing people who have been indicted and the links between them; the result is shown in figure 8.9.

We can add additional filters on the nodes and edges to run multiple filters concurrently. Imagine looking only at bank transactions between checking accounts where the amount of the transaction is between $100,000 and $475,000; that series of filters would look something like figure 8.10—notice the distribution of the property below the Range attribute, which is useful.

You can create as many filters as you like in Gephi but, as mentioned at the beginning of the chapter, you're still limited by how much data it's realistic to hold in the graph model in memory. Depending on system hardware, Gephi starts to run sluggishly when the number of nodes and links runs into the hundreds of thousands, but for anything short of that, the filter's capability helps you drill down to the areas of the data that are relevant to you.

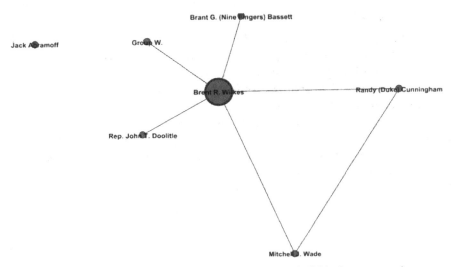

Figure 8.9 The Abramoff chart filtered to show only those individuals or companies indicted in the scandal

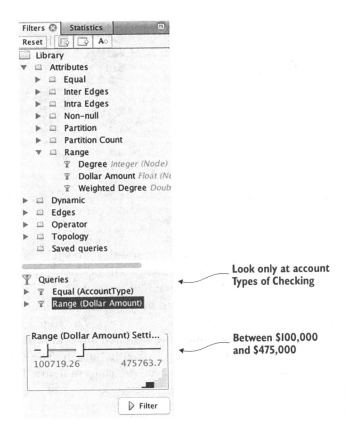

Look only at account Types of Checking

Between $100,000 and $475,000

Figure 8.10 A complex filter looking at properties of nodes and a range of values on links

8.1.2   *Filtering in KeyLines*

With KeyLines, there's no built-in UI for allowing filtering, though it has a clever API for filtering both nodes and edges. KeyLines allows you to create your own custom UI for filtering, but it requires some coding, unlike Gephi. In KeyLines, by far the most commonly used filtering capability is the ability to filter by node type, and the most common and recommended method for filtering nodes by type is with a series of check boxes in a legend that identifies the types shown on the chart. This allows the user to merely check or uncheck the box next to a specific node type to turn it on or off on the chart. I've copied figure 8.4 here in figure 8.11 to look at the airline chart, which was designed in KeyLines, and the check boxes next to the airlines to allow the user to filter down to just flights on specific airlines.

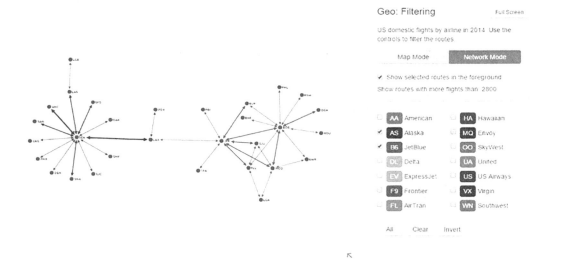

Figure 8.11   Filtering by type using check boxes in KeyLines

In this example, I also added a slider to control the range—the threshold number of flights between those city pairs in the year above which it will be shown. Checking a box or dragging the slider will rerun the filter automatically, so the user can see the results immediately. KeyLines has a basic way and an advanced way of filtering chart data. The basic way is to use `chart.hide(id, options, callback)`. This function takes a single node or link or an array of nodes and links to hide them all. `Chart.show` is the equivalent function to show nodes or links that are currently hidden. The following code sample would hide the Boston and JFK airports from the chart in figure 8.11:

```
chart.hide(['BOS','JFK'], {true, 100});
```

The `options` object allows you to animate the hiding of the objects to create a fading effect, and the `100` allows you to set the time that the transition takes.

Although they work fine, hiding and showing nodes and links individually can be a maintenance nightmare. After each check of a check box or each movement of the slider bar in the previous example, you'd have to write code to cycle through every node and link on the chart and see if it met the multiple criteria to be shown or hidden. So I use `chart.hide` in only the simplest cases. For more-complex filters, there's `chart.filter`, which is a bit tricky but powerful once you understand it.

`chart.filter()` is a function that takes as its first argument another function—one that you write that encodes the filter criteria and should return `True` if the node or link should be visible and `False` otherwise. So you'd be able to do the following to show only routes with more than 2800 flights per year:

```
chart.filter(flightFilter, {type: 'link'});          ⟵⌐  Filters only links

function flightFilter(item) {                         ⟵⌐  Function is run for each
return (item.d.numFlights > 2800);   ⟵⌐  Checks the   │   link on the chart, which
}                                        numFlights   │   gets passed in to item
                                         property
```

This function also cleans up the chart when it completes, so any node that has all its links hidden will be hidden itself, and any link that has one of its endpoints hidden will also be hidden itself.

BUILDING A FILTER USER INTERFACE

Let's go back to our Abramoff chart and add the same filter we did in Gephi to our chart, a toggle that will show only those indicted of fraud versus all of our chart data, to get a sense of how you can build these filters in KeyLines. First, we'll need to add a check box to the page itself. Let's add this to the HTML:

```
<input type=checkbox" id="indicted" value="indictedFilter">Show Only
Indicted<br>
```

And then we'll add the following to our JavaScript to run when the check box's status has been changed (checked or unchecked):

```
$('#indicted').on('change keyup', function () {
    doFiltering();
});
```

OK, this will run the `doFiltering` function, so let's write that:

```
function doFiltering() {
  chart.filter(indictmentCheck, {type: 'node'}, function() {    ⟵⌐  Filtering
    chart.layout();                                              │   nodes
  });
}
```

This passes every node to a function called indictmentCheck that we must also write, returning True if the person has been indicted and False otherwise. We use a custom property on the node's d (stands for *data*) property called indicted to check this. Key-Lines allows you to store as many custom key-value pairs on a node or link as you like.

```
function indictmentCheck(item) {
  if ($('#indicted').checked){
    return item.d.indicted;
  }
  else
    return true;
}
```

If check box is unchecked, show everything

Now you have a working filter. Checking the box will hide the nodes of items not indicted and unchecking it will show everything, as shown in figure 8.12.

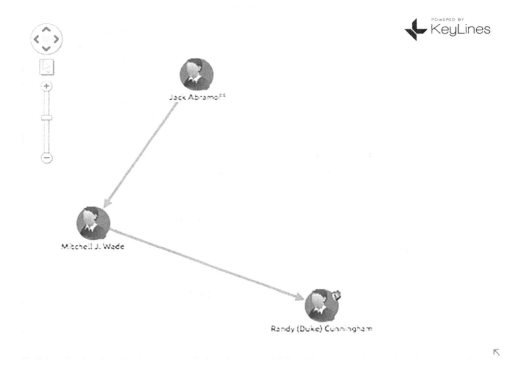

Figure 8.12   The Abramoff chart in KeyLines after the filter has been run

This method of implementing filters can be powerful, but there are some drawbacks too. If you have multiple filters, there's no way in KeyLines to stack them together as there is in Gephi; instead, you have to write the filter function to check every filter condition that you have running to determine whether the node or link should be shown or hidden. This can get complex if you have many different filters running, because any change to one of them needs to check the condition of all the others to ensure that items that are filtered out by one filter aren't shown if they pass through another filter.

Filtering can be helpful, but ultimately it's really just turning things off or on in the chart; it's not a world-changing technology. Next, we'll discuss combinations, or grouping together nodes and links, another way to present more data than is feasible when trying to draw every data endpoint on the screen.

8.2 Grouping and combinations

Often, a one-to-one correspondence between the data elements in your database and the nodes and links on the screen isn't the most useful way of visualizing a graph data set. A lot of data concerns the connections between groups of nodes, not just between individuals, and occasionally two nodes may have many relationships between them. Drawing them all just obscures any insight into the data, as in the example in figure 8.13, where a text message conversation between these two phones results in seven links.

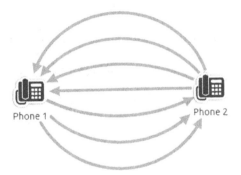

Figure 8.13 These two phones call each other a lot, and each call is represented by a single link.

What can be really useful here is to group together nodes and represent the entire group in your data with a single node on the chart. You may want to represent multiple people as a family on the chart or roll up IP addresses by subnet to look at broader trends. This allows you to get a zoomed-out or summarized view of the data instead of a granular detail. In this section, you'll learn the value of grouping and how you can create charts that show relationships between groups of entities in both Gephi and KeyLines.

8.2.1 What is grouping?

Let's return to the email data we looked at earlier in this chapter. In figures 8.1 and 8.2, reproduced in figure 8.14, we used filters to pare down the amount of data we were displaying so that we were looking at only two departments. But what if we were interested not in the individuals within each department but at how the departments themselves communicate? How do we create a graph for that?

The answer is what Gephi calls *grouping* and what KeyLines calls *combinations*. The concept involves taking groups of nodes that share a common property, such as membership

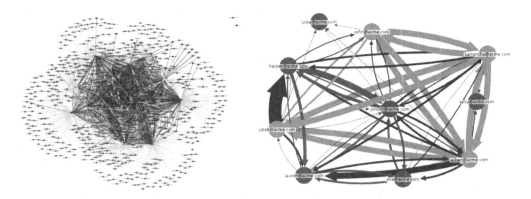

Figure 8.14   We may want to use grouping to look at how departments communicate with each other.

in a department, and drawing a single node on the chart that encompasses the entire group. The links are redrawn such that *any link originating from any member of the group is now drawn from the new node that represents the group.* So, in the email example, any email sent from any member of the marketing department will now show as being from the marketing node. This enables us to see patterns in the communications of the company's departments, ignoring the detail of the individuals, as you can see in figure 8.15.

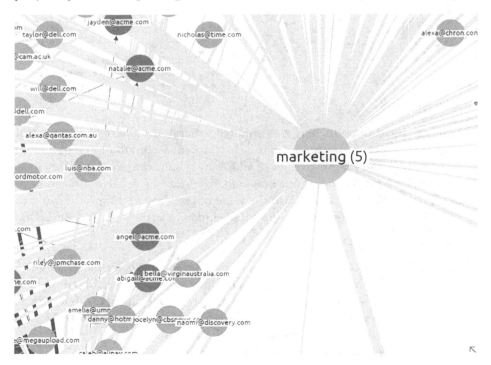

Figure 8.15   All marketing nodes are grouped together into a single node on the chart.

It's likely that we don't want to make just one group on our chart; if we're interested in communications between departments, we probably want to combine all the departments and see how they're communicating. There's no limit to the number of groups we can make on a chart, and it can occasionally be useful to create groups with just a single node; say, if the IT department was just one guy, we'd want to show his department as IT, not as an individual when every other node on the chart is a group. Let's look at the chart with all the departments combined in figure 8.16 and see if we get any useful insight that we wouldn't otherwise see.

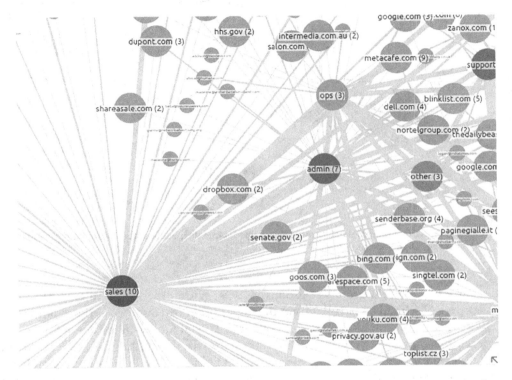

Figure 8.16 We've grouped employees in each department together so that we can see the details of which domains sales is talking to without having to see the individual salespeople.

Grouping isn't just a one-time thing. Because graphs are interactive, you can group and ungroup at will, exploring the detail of one group on the chart while leaving the others summarized for context. This is powerful because it gives your user a drill-down capability that allows them to get more insight. Let's expand just the sales group in this chart and leave everything else combined; the result is shown in figure 8.17. Notice that we can see individual salespeople and their communication patterns, but we aren't drowning in all the other data that may not be relevant to us.

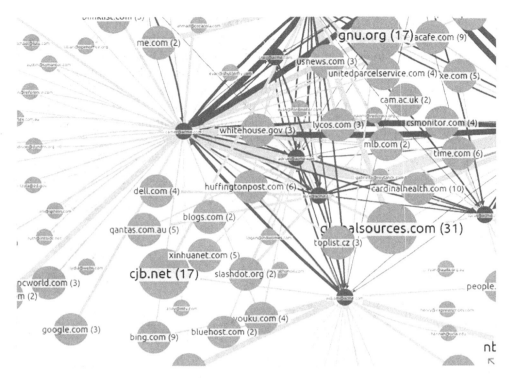

Figure 8.17 External domains are still grouped, but salespeople are split into individual nodes, allowing us to see the detail.

We can even do groups of groups, or a recursive process. We might want to take the previous email chart and group the departments themselves, perhaps putting marketing and sales in a commercial node and IT and admin in an operations node. This would give us a very zoomed-out or summarized view, but the user could still drill down to the individual data elements. But be careful! A node can be a member of only one group or else you'll run into logical problems. This may not be immediately obvious; why couldn't an employee be a member of both sales and marketing? But what happens when the sales group is expanded; do you draw that person? Probably yes, but that individual is also still on the chart in the grouped form as a member of the marketing group, so links to that person would go to both the individual and groups. And having the same node on the chart twice can lead to lots of confusion, so be careful here.

Let's look at one more example and return to the terrorism data that we discussed in chapter 2. There we were looking at data of intercepted communications between individual terrorists, and we drew a graph that showed each person on the chart using the flag of the country where they lived. Figure 8.18 shows the chart again.

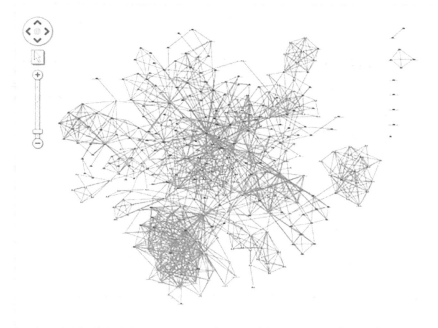

Figure 8.18 The terrorism chart from chapter 2. It's cluttered and hard to understand what's going on.

Grouping can help us better understand this data. Let's take everybody from a single country and group them together; then the resulting node will represent the entire country. Now we have a more geopolitical view of the terrorist networks. I sized the node and used the glyph to indicate the number of individuals in each country, and I also sized the width of the link to show the number of communications between people in those countries. This provides a different level of analysis; there's nothing in the data that shows how many people from Saudi Arabia are talking to people from Malaysia. It's only at the grouped level that these insights become possible. The image is shown in figure 8.19.

And the recursive process works here too—maybe we want to take the countries themselves and group them by region to get a summarized view of the data. But of course, the drill-down capability is still there, so as an end user, if I'm an analyst focused on a specific country, I can expand just that group, the members of that country, and leave the rest intact, as shown in figure 8.20 with Turkey.

Although possible with clever queries, grouping isn't practical to do at the database level, but both Gephi and KeyLines have the ability to do this grouping within the visualization itself. Let's look at how to implement it.

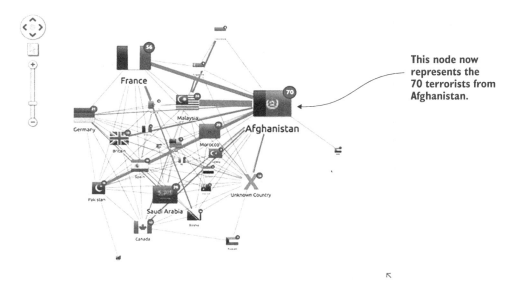

This node now represents the 70 terrorists from Afghanistan.

Figure 8.19   The terrorism chart with all the countries grouped into single nodes

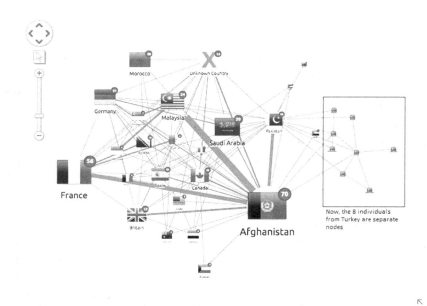

Now, the 8 individuals from Turkey are separate nodes

Figure 8.20   The detail for Turkey extracted while leaving everybody else grouped

8.2.2 Grouping in Gephi

WARNING! Although grouping was available in Gephi .08X beta, which was the most recent version when this chapter was initially written, the latest stable release, 0.9, does not contain the grouping capability. This is a disappointment, and I'm leaving the rest of the section intact in the hope that it will soon return.

Creating groups in Gephi is very easy and can be done from both the overview window and the data laboratory. You can select multiple nodes in the overview window by using the marquee selection tool on the left side of the window and dragging it around a number of different nodes. Then right-click anywhere and a context menu will appear with the option to group those nodes. Gephi does all the work of removing the selected nodes, replacing them with a node for the entire group, and rerouting the links to the new destination. It works well, but Gephi doesn't make it easy to see what's selected when working from the overview window, and you can't select multiple nodes from different parts of your screen (you'd think Shift-click would work, but it doesn't). See the example in figure 8.21.

Figure 8.21 Grouping in Gephi is done by selecting nodes and choosing Group from a context menu.

That's why I think it's easier to use grouping from the data laboratory. In the data lab, the nodes are displayed in tabular format, and multi-select works just fine, so you can click to select multiple rows and then right-click to group them. The group itself will now appear as a node in the list, so recursion works here too; you can now select that node and others to make a group of groups. Ungrouping, or drilling down, is also accessed by right-clicking.

8.2.3 Grouping in KeyLines

In KeyLines, grouping is done with the chart.combo() namespace. As with the other features we've discussed, there's no UI, so it's up to you how you want to allow the user to combine nodes: with a button, a context menu, or anything else you might decide is useful. chart.combo().combine takes an object called a combo definition, which has the visual properties of the group node and an array of node IDs that compose the group. If you want to create multiple groups with one function call, you can pass an array of combo definitions to the combine function. Here's an example:

```
chart.combo().combine({ids:['1','2'], label: 'group of two'});
```

This will take both nodes with the IDs 1 and 2 and combine them in a group. The new node will have the same style as node 1 (though this can be customized) and have the label "group of two."

Some other important functions in the combo namespace are isCombo(), which returns True if the node passed in is a combo and False otherwise, and uncombine(), which will take the ID of a combo node and break it into its original pieces.

Let's add the capability on our Abramoff chart to create combos by selecting multiple items and clicking a button. First, as in our other examples, we need to add a couple of buttons to our HTML page:

```
<button id="combine">Combine</button>
<button id="uncombine">Uncombine</button>
```

And then we need to add a handler to the button in our JavaScript:

```
$('#combine').click(combineSelected);          ◁———  Runs combineSelected
$('#uncombine').click(uncombineSelected);              function when the
                                                       button is clicked
function combineSelected(){
  chart.combo().combine({
    ids: chart.selection()
  });
}
function uncombineSelected(){
  chart.combo().uncombine(chart.selection());
}
```

The result is shown in figure 8.22.

When building an application using KeyLines, it's helpful to give users the abilities to filter, group, and ungroup at will. This way, they can view the data at the level that's the most interesting to them. In the next chapter, we'll look at what to do when you want to understand how data changes over time and how to visualize that.

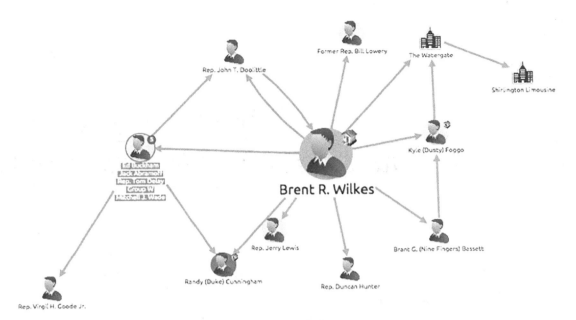

Figure 8.22   Several nodes of the Abramoff chart grouped together in KeyLines

8.3   *Summary*

In this chapter, you learned the following:

- Unless your data set is really small, trying to render the whole thing in one visualization isn't helpful.
- Filter on the visualization side for user control; filter on the database side for performance.
- Filtering the data on the database side is critical if you're working with a very large data set, because you can't expect KeyLines, Gephi, or any other tool to hold that much data in memory.
- Filtering smaller sets via the visualizations UI can be helpful in giving the user the ability to understand the details of the data elements that interest them.
- Grouping can be a helpful way of reducing clutter, and allowing the user to drill down to inspect the detail can promote a deeper understanding of the data.
- Gephi allows you to select individual rows in the data laboratory and group them together.
- KeyLines has a combo namespace that contains a number of combination functions.

Dynamic graphs:
how to show data over time

This chapter covers

- How to present data when it has a date/time element
- What to do with data that changes over time
- How to deal with graph elements that contain durations

So far, one of the major themes of this book is that although static graph visualizations are good, interactivity is far better. Allowing for interaction with graph visualizations offers an additional element that significantly enhances the user experience and the ease by which viewers can gain valuable information about the data contained in the graph. In a sense, those interactive graph visualizations are *dynamic* in that the user can control what they're seeing by laying out the data differently or applying filters. That's not what I talk about in this chapter. Here, when I say *dynamic graphs*, I mean graphs where the data itself is changing over time, such as when you're looking at financial transactions (cash transfers between bank accounts, for example) or census information (such as migration patterns of human movements between countries). How do you show graphs over time? You need to figure out exactly what that means, and there are two scenarios where you might want to do this:

- Visualizing how you changed your graph over time. (What new data did you add to your graph, and when did you add it?)
- Visualizing graph data that has some sort of date/time property. (How do you illustrate dates and times in your data?)

In the first instance, it might be important to know when and where you added data to your graph. Imagine you're an intelligence analyst and you're attempting to justify going to war in Iraq in 2003. You need to show a graph of what was known about Iraq intelligence at the time, leaving out all the data that became known later. The date/time associated with each graph item (node or edge) might be the point in time at which that item was added to your graph data, so in effect you have a history of your graph and how it evolved as you added new data.

The second instance is where there's a date/time property on your data itself. This could be on the nodes but is far more often found on the links. In chapter 1 of this book, we made a graph of the Enron emails, showing who was emailing whom. At the time, we didn't pay attention to when those emails were sent, but each email, which we modeled as a link between the sender and the receiver, has a date/time associated with it, as do most communications data or transactional data. Now I can show you how to visualize that date/time data.

In both of these instances, we're interested not only in the what—what's connected to what else; that's adequately covered in the node-link diagrams—but also the when—when did those connections happen? How do we show that, and do important patterns emerge?

9.1 How do graphs change over time?

Before we get into how to visualize data that has a time element, we have to think about what we gain from visualizing this data. What sorts of things would an effective time-based graph visualization show? In short, why do we care? Table 9.1 shows some examples.

Table 9.1 A list of ways graphs can change over time and why those changes might be relevant to see

Graph change	Relevance	Example
Node addition and removal	Perhaps nodes were relevant in your graph for only a short duration of time.	In graphing IP traffic, it's useful to see if an IP address had a brief flurry of activity and then went silent, possibly indicating the device was turned off.
Link addition and removal	Perhaps two nodes were connected for only a short duration of time and unrelated otherwise.	If you're looking at criminal networks, two criminals may have communicated directly at first but now go through intermediaries.
Property changes on nodes or links	Perhaps properties that are relevant are increasing or decreasing over time.	In graphing financial networks, perhaps a bank account started out small but grew significantly over time and is now worthy of more scrutiny.

Table 9.1   A list of ways graphs can change over time and why those changes might be relevant to see *(continued)*

Graph change	Relevance	Example
Community formation or dissolution	Perhaps groups of nodes are tightly connected at times but unrelated otherwise.	When graphing social networks, social groups often start off homogenous with lots of links between them but quickly split off into isolated groups.

In most networks, the time attribute is on the link, not the node. Let's look at a couple of examples:

- In a financial network, when listing transactions between merchants and customers, each transaction has a time stamp, and there can be several (for example, when an individual buys from a merchant several times over the course of a day). In this case, the time we care about is the time of those transactions that are the links in our network. We might be interested in uncovering patterns in the timing of those transactions from a business intelligence perspective to learn more about who was buying products and when. Figure 9.1 shows an example of this.

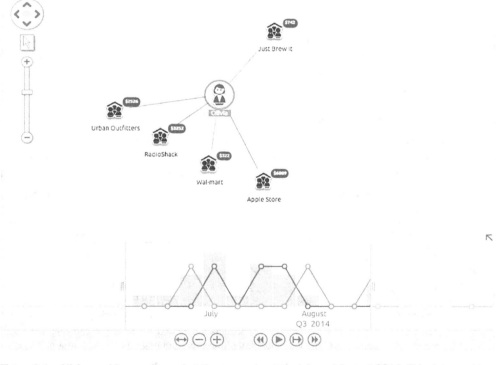

Figure 9.1   Olivia used her credit card at these merchants in July and August 2014. This data could be important in understanding how stolen credit card numbers propagate by looking at the pattern of disputed transactions.

- In the review fraud example we explored in chapter 2, we looked at Amazon reviews of products and tried to uncover the patterns that appear when someone submits fraudulent reviews, namely, false positive reviews of themselves and false negative reviews of their competitors. In that example, we neglected to mention the time variable, but it's a critical element when trying to uncover suspicious behavior. Did these reviews happen all at once within a short time span, or were they spread out over months or years? Because the review is the link between the reviewer and the product, those dates and times will appear as properties on the link. Figure 9.2 has an example of this.

- Communications networks also will almost certainly have a date/time stamp on the link, regardless of the method of communication. Whether you're tracking emails, text messages, or phone calls, each one of those communications happens at a particular date and time, and it's helpful to understand not just that Sam emailed Holly but when. I show examples of this in section 9.2.2.

Sometimes it isn't enough to know that a relationship exists between nodes; in some cases, better analysis is possible if you can also visualize when the relationship took place. Because relationships are denoted with links between nodes, the date/time data appears as a property of the link.

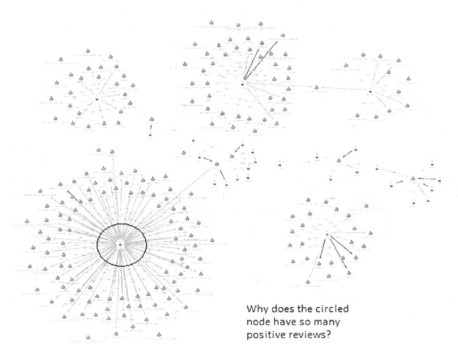

Why does the circled node have so many positive reviews?

Figure 9.2 **The user at the lower left has left dozens of five-star reviews and no negative ones. If those reviews are spread over time, perhaps the user is just easy to satisfy. If they came all at once, it's more likely the user is a bot or part of an astroturfing campaign.**

Now let's look at different techniques for visualizing time-based data.

9.2 *How to visualize changes over time*

There are countless different approaches to visualizing dynamic graphs; an entire subdomain of graph theory is dedicated to it. I've selected two of the most popular approaches to discuss here alongside some examples of when they're useful. The small multiples approach is helpful when you want to see the change of the graph structure over time but don't necessarily need to see the detail of individual nodes and links. The time bar approach gives the user control over which window of time they want to view but doesn't present the data all on one page and therefore requires more effort.

9.2.1 *Small multiples—showing time with many small graphs*

One method for showing changes over time is to show a completely separate graph for a number of time instants. This can be helpful to show changes in the structure of the graph over time, but in order to show a large number of graphs, they would have to be quite small to fit on a single page. This makes identifying the exact items that are changing very difficult.

Let's look at an example, shown in figure 9.3. This series of graphs shows the increasing polarization of the US Congress over the last few decades, as seen in the voting history of each member of the House of Representatives. The graph shows each elected representative as a node, with the color indicating their party affiliation and the links between nodes the instances where those people voted together on a bill. This graphic originally appeared in the journal *PLOS One* (Public Library of Science) in April 2015. Notice that the changes in the structure of the graph are readily apparent; in the 1950s and 1960s, there were lots of Democrats voting with lots of Republicans, but bipartisanship has all but disappeared in more recent years. But what we don't see in this graph is any information about individual members of Congress and how they voted—those details are lost because the value of the graph is in showing the change in structure. This is OK for the point the authors are trying to prove in this visualization, but it wouldn't work if the goal were to see how individual members of Congress were voting alongside their colleagues.

It becomes easy to spot when the makeup of Congress leaned more heavily Democrat (blue) or Republican (red). It also shows times when major national events influenced the likelihood that representatives would vote across party lines, like in 2001 when Democrats and Republicans voted together to pass tougher national security measures in the wake of the September 11 attacks.

Figure 9.3   Many small graphs showing decreased collaboration between members of Congress of different parties over time. Look at the difference between the 1993 makeup of Congress and that of 1995: many more Republicans were elected, and it marked a shift to a time when collaboration between the parties has all but ended. This diagram is included in the color section in the print edition of this book.

9.2.2 *Time-based filtering*

The best approach under most circumstances, and a feature included with both Key-Lines and Gephi, is to allow filtering by time on a single node-link visualization. This means that instead of showing different charts on individual slices of time, the user selects a window of time and thus filters the chart to show only the events that happened during that window. The drawback of this approach is that it doesn't allow for a big-picture single view that allows you to see how the network changes over time and therefore isn't possible with static diagrams, but in interactive environments, it works well.

A SAMPLE OF APPLYING FILTERS TO THE NODOBO DATA SET

Let's look at an example of high schoolers' cell phone use. In 2010, researchers at the University of Strathclyde in Scotland conducted a study on cell phone use in which they visited a high school class and gave each student a Google Nexus smartphone. The students could use the phones for the duration of the semester, on the condition that the researchers could track the students' interactions on those phones. The purpose of the study was to better understand how teenagers interact with their cell phones, but the researchers made all the data publicly available (properly anonymized) in what's known as the Nodobo data set. Because each phone call or text message is a transaction between two phones, we can use this data to create a graph of the communications made by these students. Let's look at this graph as a standard node-link diagram in figure 9.4.

The result of the study was that over the course of five months in 2010–11, the researchers gathered records of 13,000 phone calls and 85,000 text messages. (Due to the volume of the data, the graph shows only a small percentage of those items. A link represents the entire relationship between two phones, which could be thousands of text messages or a single phone call. This makes for a manageable diagram.)

We can learn some social patterns by looking at who is communicating with whom. The well-connected nodes at the center of the chart are the students who are calling and texting their peers the most. The nodes around the perimeter of the graph aren't as socially connected. Figure 9.5 is a view with more detail.

This diagram tells us nothing about when those connections happen, though. Do the phone calls spike on weekends or in the evenings? Is the overall trend up or down? What about calls during the holiday break; how is that graph different from the graph showing all the calls? In order to answer that, we need to use the interactivity of the graph to explore different windows of time. A common technique for this is to use a time slider and a filter. Figure 9.6 shows what the slider would look like, and figure 9.7 shows the filter.

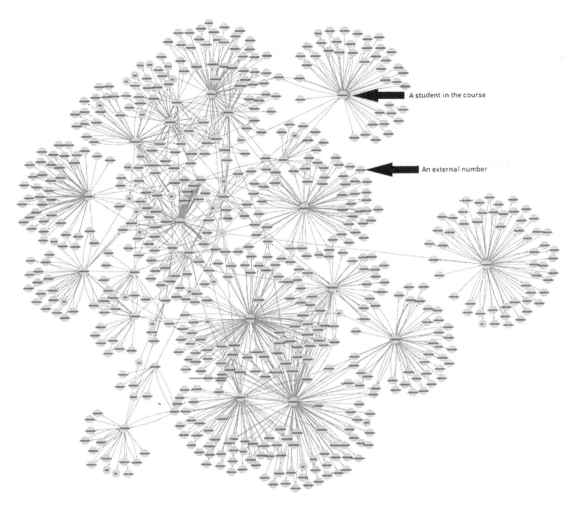

A student in the course

An external number

Figure 9.4 A graph of the students' phone calls in the Nodobo study. The nodes at the center of the starburst patterns are the students themselves and the isolated nodes surrounding them are the phones they called. When the starbursts are connected, it means two students in the study contacted each other. Most of the numbers the students called were not a part of the study, however (say, when they called a pizza parlor or their parents).

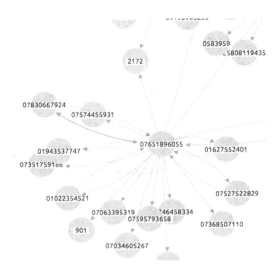

Figure 9.5   More detail from the Nodobo
data set displayed in figure 9.4. The study
participants appear in the center of each
starburst. Links are either unidirectional
or bidirectional, indicating whether the
participant sent or received calls and texts.
(The phone numbers are anonymized, which is
why they don't appear as normal numbers.)

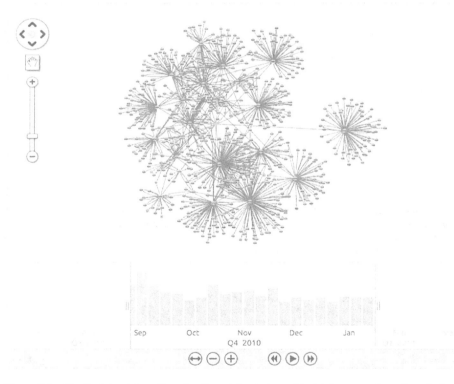

Figure 9.6   The Nodobo data with a timeline at the bottom. The histograms show the relative
frequency of communications in each time period from September 2010 to January 2011, with spikes
in early September and the end of October.

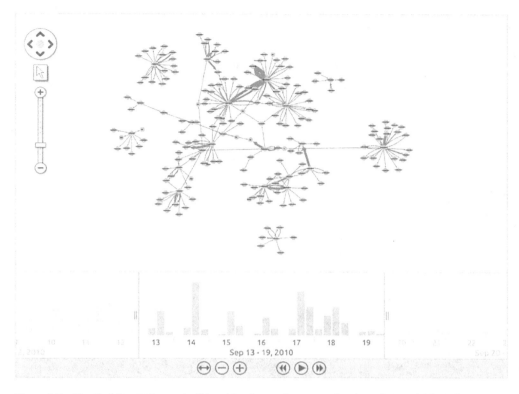

Figure 9.7   The Nodobo study graph, filtered to show only communications that took place the second week of September

The time bar you see in the bottom of figure 9.6 is a simple bar chart. The height of the bars shows the frequency of communications during that time window, showing a peak at the beginning of the semester when the students are excited to get a new phone, a trough in October when they realize it's just another phone like any other, and then another spike around Halloween. It levels off after that. This is useful information, but it's not particularly relevant to the graph. The better analysis comes in when we zoom and pan on the time bar. Let's zoom in on the second week of September, where there's a spike in activity; you'll see this in figure 9.7.

In addition to zooming the time bar and changing the units from weeks to days on the bar chart, the chart is also filtered to hide all the links (and the nodes that as a result would have no links). What we can see in this week is that there are a number of isolated subgraphs that aren't connected to each other—students are communicating with external phone numbers but not among themselves as much. That's expected for the very beginning of the course, before the students have gotten to know their classmates. Let's zoom in one more time to see September 14, 2010, because it's a very active day in the study. Figure 9.8 shows the details.

Figure 9.8   Filtering to display only communications on September 14, 2010, divided by hour on the time bar. The graph shows that nearly all the calls happened in the afternoon and that the graph is very broken up—the students aren't talking to each other much at all.

What we see at this level of detail is the frequency of calls by hour of the day, and the graph shows that there's very little communication between students, as you can see from the broken up nature of the graph. You can create interactivity on the time bar just as you can interact with the chart (zooming in or panning). It allows you to see how the chart changes when you apply those filters, watching as nodes appear and disappear. Patterns over time become evident, such as how students are calling each other more often in the evenings versus calling external numbers in the daytime.

You'll also notice a Play button at the bottom of the time bar in figure 9.8. Both KeyLines and Gephi provide the ability to animate time and show the changes identified in table 9.1. The animation shows nodes and links appearing and disappearing as they fall inside and out of the time window.

When you apply filters based on time to this data set, you can see student communications peak around key events. By pinpointing a specific time of interest, the filters can show you patterns of the students' communication activity and how that changes over time. Next, we'll look at what happens when events last longer than an instant.

Please note

We've treated these communications examples as being a single instant in time, say 2:15:00 p.m. on February 15, 2015, EDT. Although this is true for text messages, it's not technically true for phone calls, because they start at a certain time, last for some number of minutes, and then end. The charts in figures 9.6–9.8 don't show that effectively. KeyLines doesn't handle this well; it treats all nodes with a date/time as having a stamp, or an instant in time. Gephi's dynamic model is more fully fleshed out, because it allows items to have both a start time and a stop time, showing that a call started at a specific time, the users talked for some amount of time, and then it ended. Zooming far in on the time bar would show calls that were *in progress* during the window of time selected, not just ones that started during that window. It's a subtle but important difference. In order to enable durations on the temporal model in Gephi, you'll need to enable time intervals, found on the configuration window in the data laboratory. We'll return to this concept in section 9.4.

9.2.3 *Graphs with dynamic properties*

At the bottom of table 9.1, I mentioned dynamic properties (property changes on nodes or links). This is a very different type of dynamic graph. Instead of the node or link having a date/time associated with it, a property of that node or link changes over time. Imagine a person is a node on a chart and he has a property of Marital Status. The value for that property is Married, but that doesn't tell the whole story. In truth, the value for that person was Single from birth to 2009 and Married thereafter. If I'm designing my graph to indicate marital status (perhaps with a node color or a glyph), I'm going to want to use the time bar to show that person as single when zoomed into a pre-2009 date and married afterward.

This is another area where Gephi allows you to visualize this but KeyLines does not. In Gephi, all date/time ranges are properties; there's no such thing as a date/time property on the node or link itself. Then you use the various features of Gephi to control how the graph visualization should appear. In chapter 5, we talked about how the partition feature allows you to assign colors to unique values of properties on nodes and links (maybe one color for married and another for single), and the rank feature allows you to scale the size or color of a node or link for numeric values of properties. Gephi doesn't care if this is a static or dynamic variable; it will automatically size/color the node appropriately based on the time selected. Animating the time bar in Gephi will show changes to visual properties as time flows, so you'd see that node flip from single to married after 2009. Filters are handled the same way; you can apply a filter in Gephi the same way you learned in chapter 6, and items will appear or disappear based on whether their value of the selected property meets the filter criteria.

Time property in KeyLines versus Gephi

There's an important distinction between the way KeyLines handles date/times and how Gephi handles them.

In KeyLines, the graph nodes and links have instants of time and the user selects a range of time to show all items that fall in that range. A node or link has one or more date/time properties on it, and each one can have a *value*. (For example, a bank transaction may have a specific date/time and a dollar amount value associated with it.) The time bar itself selects a range, and KeyLines is often customized to filter the chart.

Gephi assigns either a time stamp or both start and stop date/times to either the node or link itself or an individual property of the node or link, allowing you to model how properties of the items are changing over time. Gephi can be customized to filter or change the size or color of nodes and links as those properties change.

9.3   *Implementing dynamic graphs*

Both KeyLines and Gephi offer methods for handling dynamic graphs. Gephi's version has more capabilities than what KeyLines can do in this regard, but it can be a bit more challenging to wrap your head around.

9.3.1   *Dynamic graphs in Gephi*

The first step is to get the right data model. Probably the best way to understand how Gephi handles dynamic data is to generate a random dynamic graph and then look at the data that was created. You can do this from the File menu: File > Generate > Dynamic Graph Example, which will use random data to create a graph. If you now go to the data laboratory to inspect the resulting data, you'll see that each node has a time stamp value indicating when that node is present. Mine looks like this:

<[2003.0, 2006.0, 2007.0, 2008.0, 2009.0]>

This shows me that this node was present in years 2003, 2006, 2007, 2008, and 2009 but was missing in all other years.

DYNAMIC FILTERING

Now this won't automatically filter the graph when the time bar is moved; to do that you have to apply a filter. Drag the Time Interval filter at the right side of the Gephi window down to the Queries panel at the bottom. This applies a filter so that only nodes and links that have a date/time that falls in the range selected are visible when the time bar is scrolled. You can see this in figure 9.9.

The time bar at the bottom of the screen now allows you to define a range that you want to select. You can size, drag, and animate this time bar to view the graph for different windows of time. You can see this in figure 9.10.

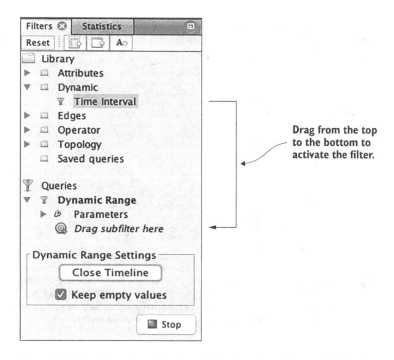

Figure 9.9   How to apply a time-based filter to a dynamic graph in Gephi

Figure 9.10   An example of the Gephi time bar. Dates are along the top. Drag the box to pan through time, and drag the edges of the box to resize the window of time. The Play button on the left will animate the graph when clicked.

DYNAMIC SIZING AND COLORING

Another feature of Gephi is that the date/time property on an item may have a value associated with it, allowing you to control not just whether that item is shown or hidden but the size and/or color of the node or link as well. Imagine a node represents a bank account, whose total account holdings vary over time. It could be useful to size the node according to how much is in that account at any one point and then use the time bar to watch it grow and shrink. To do that, there's a slightly different way of storing the data. Instead of just a list of time stamps, you need a list of time stamps alongside their associated values. The dynamic graph example shows this also, under a table called Score. In my case, it looks like this:

<[2003.0, 4]; [2006.0, 1]; [2008.0, 2]; [2009.0, 1]; [2012.0, 1]; [2013.0, 4]>

This means that in 2003 the value of this node was 4, in 2006 it was 1, and so on. Let's assign that property to the size of the node. This is done from the Appearance pane in the upper-left side of the window. I've shown this in figure 9.11.

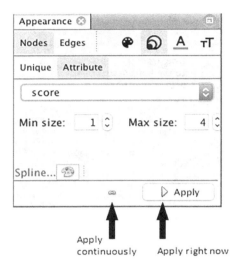

Figure 9.11 **Assigning the node size to the value of the score property enables the node to grow or shrink as you move through the time bar. The unlabeled button at the bottom center of the chart switches to dynamic mode.**

Clicking Apply will automatically scale the size of the node according to the score attribute as it appears right now. Alternatively, the chain link icon in the bottom center of the dialog (which I highlighted with an arrow in figure 9.11 so you don't miss it) will switch to continuous mode, where it will resize nodes based on their value at the time that appears in the time bar. Try this and then animate the time bar; you'll watch nodes grow and shrink as their values change. (You can also change the maximum size to 15 to make the differences more obvious.)

DYNAMIC LAYOUTS

Another feature of dynamic graphs in Gephi is the ability to run layouts continuously—this means that as the graph changes over time, you can run a new layout with each tick of the time bar, making the chart easier to read as nodes and links appear and disappear. Only a few of the layouts in the Layouts pane support this continuous mode, the main ones being ForceAtlas, ForceAtlas2, and Fruchterman-Reingold. Those layouts will continue to run when selected, and as changes happen in the chart because of changes in the time bar, the layout will reorganize the chart. This can be helpful if otherwise you'd have widely disparate items because everything in between was hidden, but it can cause confusion and the user can lose their place if things are continuously flying around. I'd shy away from using this too often, but it is useful on graphs with few nodes.

9.3.2 *Dynamic graphs in KeyLines*

KeyLines handles dates and times a bit differently from Gephi—the basic idea of having a time bar allowing users to scroll through and animate time is the same, but date/times are strictly properties of the node or link. Dates and times can't be applied to a property of a node or link, and they're solely time stamps, not durations with start and end times. This limits the applicability to cases where the user is interested in analyzing patterns in instantaneous events or where viewing the duration isn't important. If you think back to the married/single example in section 9.3.2, you'll recall that KeyLines can't show changes in properties over time, so you can't graph this information because marital status is a property of a node.

DATA MODEL

KeyLines has a special property on each node and link called `dt`, and this is part of the JSON object model that defines chart items. Because KeyLines is JavaScript, it uses the JavaScript date object to assign date/times, but epoch time (the number of seconds since January 1, 1970) is also supported. JavaScript has a decent date parser too, so something like "July 3rd, 2015, 3pm GMT" would correctly parse to epoch time, which can then be passed to KeyLines. Chart items can have more than one date/time also, which is important because in the text message example I showed earlier, the link represents the entire conversation, which includes many dozen individual messages, each of which has its own time stamp. Each time stamp can optionally have a value, similar to Gephi, but this value must be a number. This value controls how the item affects the histograms. If it exists, the height of the histogram is the sum total of the values in that time range (useful for bank transactions, for example, where the amount being transferred is more important than the total number of transactions). An example of a JSON object containing a date/time follows:

```
{
id: 'Corey',
type: 'node',
dt: [1457374912, 1457141521],      ◁─┐ Multiple date/
c: 'blue',                              time stamps
e: 1.5
}
```

This can apply to nodes, edges, or both.

BUILDING A CHART

Once you have your JSON data object, you can pass the data to KeyLines to build your chart. In KeyLines, the node-link chart and the time bar are two separate HTML components, but they take the same data and can be bound together. So you pass the same JSON object to both `chart.load()` and `timebar.load()`. Now you have two components with the same data, but there's no interoperability between the two. Similar to the way chart events in KeyLines can be bound to JavaScript functions, the same is true with the time bar. So click, hover, and change are all events that fire when the user interacts with the time bar. Change also fires when the range of the time bar has been changed by animation. What you want to do is have the node-link chart filter to show only the items in a selected window of time in the time bar—that's just a few lines of code:

Filter to only the items in the time bar's range

Bind the time bar changes to the filter function on the chart

```
timebar.bind('change', function () {
chart.filter(timebar.inRange, { animate: false, type: 'link' }, function() {
chart.layout('tweak', { animate: true, time: 1000 });
});
```

Run a layout after each change; the tweaked layout slightly alters the position of nodes as opposed to redrawing the entire chart.

By decoupling the time bar from the chart, you could choose to do other things to the chart as the user interacts with the time bar. Replacing `chart.filter()` with `chart.background()` in the previous code would gray out items that fall outside the selected range instead of hiding them altogether. You could also change the visual styling of items during certain time ranges by using `chart.setProperties`. Another thing that can be helpful with the time bar change event is that you may want to load your data into the chart piecemeal as opposed to all at once. One strategy would be to re-query your data source when the user scrolls the time bar outside the initial range to obtain that new data and populate the chart:

```
function adjustData() {
var range = timebar.range();
var t1 = range.dt1.getTime();
var t2 = range.dt2.getTime();

var needToFetch = t1 < originalFrom || t2 > originalTo;

if(needToFetch){
fetchData(t1, t2, dataRangeFrom, dataRangeTo);
}
}
```

timebar.range gives two endpoints of range

Compare to original values to see if you need to fetch new data

fetchData would be function to access your data source but isn't defined here

The chart in figure 9.12 shows an example. The data is from the Boston Hubway system, where users can rent a bicycle at one location in the city and return it to another location later that day.

This is modeled as a graph with the stations as nodes and the trips taken by cyclists as links. The time of each trip is shown on the time bar, showing a diurnal pattern (lots of daytime trips and almost none at night), as expected. In this case, the time bar's range is bound to the filter function of the chart, therefore showing only trips taken during the selected window, but also the node's color is bound to the number of rentals originating or terminating at that station during the selected time window. As the time bar animates, links will appear and disappear and the nodes will change color depending on how busy they are.

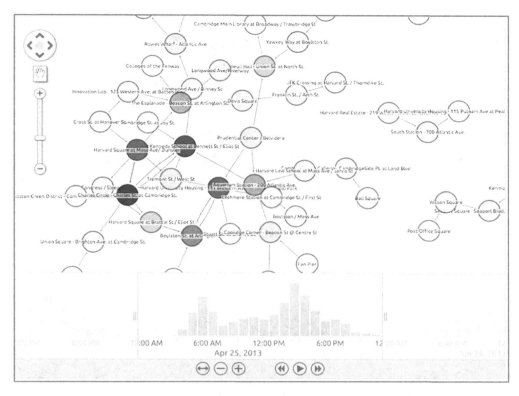

Figure 9.12 A graph showing short-term bike rentals in Boston, MA. Dark stations are high traffic and light stations are lower traffic. The time bar shows the window of time we're considering.

SELECTIONS

The time bar histograms aren't labeled with values, so the absolute height of those bars is somewhat meaningless. They're useful only to get a *relative* understanding of the frequency of items in the time window. The same is true for selection lines, which are a way of showing subsets of the graph on the time bar. Often, it's useful to look at a small sample of the data and see how it compares to the full data to see if there are similar patterns. For example, we may want to look at how a particular person's communications compare to all the communications in our data set. To do this, the time bar allows us to specify what KeyLines calls a *selection object* on it, which shows a line graph in a specific color. Figure 9.13 has an example.

The green line is a selection object selecting just the bike trips that originated at the Harvard Square station and the red line shows those that terminate at Harvard Square. The result is that we can suss out patterns over time of different subsets of the data; are more bikes being rented at certain stations in the morning and returned in the evenings or the other way around? The selection object is easy to

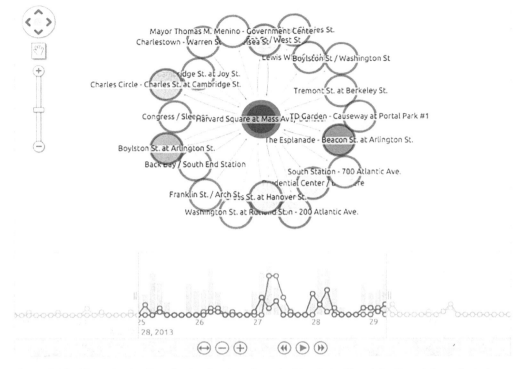

Figure 9.13   The selection lines in the time bar show the bicycle traffic originating at the selected station (green) and terminating at that station (red). This could aid the organization in learning when bikes must be manually moved from one station to another so there are always enough bikes where they are needed.

assemble; it's just an array of the IDs of the items you want highlighted, along with some options:

```
var items = [
  {id: ['id1', 'id2'], index: 0, c: 'green'},     ⟵  Selection line 1 in green
  {id: ['id3', 'id4'], index: 1, c: 'red' }        ⟵  Selection line 2 in red
];
timebar.selection(items);
```

KeyLines allows up to three selection objects per chart.

Gephi and KeyLines have different strengths in graphing dynamic data. Gephi has more features, allowing more fine-tuned control over the time data. KeyLines has a blunter data model but is easier to implement.

9.4 *Summary*

In this chapter, you learned the following:

- Graph data is nearly always changing. You can use small multiple graphs or time bars to visualize those changes.
- You should nearly always add date/time stamps as a property of the link instead of the node.
- Time bars allow you to filter the graph to show only the data that occurred during a selected time window.
- Filtering by time helps you understand patterns in the data.
- In Gephi, you can make properties dynamic instead of using time stamps on nodes and links. This way you can model different values for properties at different times.
- KeyLines adds a date/time property to both nodes and links and allows the same data model in both the graph and the time bar. They have to be linked together to do filtering.

In this chapter, we looked at how graph data can change over time and how you can make better, dynamic graphs to answer the "when" question. In the next chapter we'll look at strategies for answering the "where." Superimposing graphs on maps can be valuable but has its own unique set of challenges.

Graphs on maps: the where of graph visualization

This chapter covers

- How to display geographic data
- The pros and cons of showing graphs on maps
- Implementing graphs and maps in KeyLines

Data visualization is about using data to answer questions. "How are these people connected?" "Who is connected to whom else?" "When did those connections happen?" are examples. In chapter 9, we talked about strategies for answering the *when* question, and now we'll work through how to answer the *where*. Unsurprisingly, to figure out where things happened, we need to use maps. So, the short answer is to put your graph on a map where the position of the nodes corresponds to the geographic location of those nodes, but it's often not that simple. In this final chapter, I'll walk through some strategies for visualizing graph data when there's a location component to it and show some hypothetical situations where there isn't yet a good solution. By the end of the chapter, you'll have some strategies for what to show when your graph data include locations.

10.1 Working with geographical data

Almost all data has a geographical component to it, because when you graph information about objects, those objects exist somewhere and have a position. A person lives somewhere, works somewhere, and travels between places. Traditional graph representation doesn't show any of this because it wasn't designed to represent locations. But graphing locations can reveal important insights in certain scenarios. In this section we'll discuss where the geographical information should live in your graph model and how that can affect how it's visualized.

10.1.1 *Graphs with location data*

Locations are often embedded in graph data, and the data from some of the examples we've looked at throughout the book contains location information that we ignored. Sometimes, however, visualizing the location data can give you insight into patterns in your data. For example, in the fraud example from chapter 2, we looked at a simplified stolen credit card scenario where we modeled transactions between cardholders and merchants. In that scenario, each merchant (in a brick-and-mortar store) has a location, and it would be interesting to see if instances of stolen cards cluster in a specific city or neighborhood. For e-commerce merchants, goods are often shipped to physical addresses, which can also be modeled with location information. Often, you're looking for clustering—instances where more than one node are grouped together geographically, which is information you wouldn't know by looking at the graph directly.

10.1.2 *How to model locations in a graph*

Remember our airline example from chapter 8, graphing city pairs in the United States and the airlines that fly those routes? In figure 10.1, I show all the airlines, but I now show only the 100 highest-passenger-volume routes in the United States.

You can see the three New York airports circled on the graph: LaGuardia (LGA), Newark (EWR), and JFK. There's no indication that these airports are all within 30 miles of each other, and without knowing geography, someone looking at this graph wouldn't have any indication either. But we can attach the location as a property of the node, because each airport in this example has an actual location in space. In this example, we'll use the latitude and longitude of the airport, so the list of properties of a node might look something like table 10.1.

Table 10.1   A list of potential properties on LaGuardia Airport

Property	Value
Node ID	LGA
Label	LGA
Name	New York LaGuardia Airport
State	New York
Latitude	40.777
Longitude	-73.872

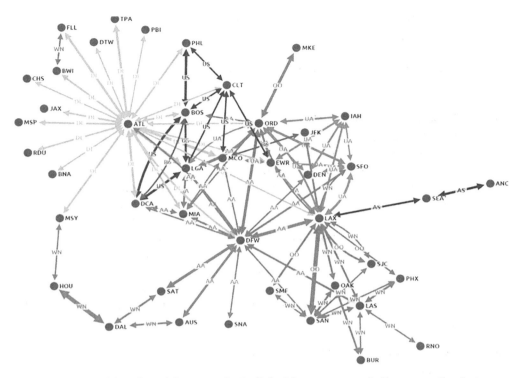

Figure 10.1   The 100 busiest airline routes in the United States as a graph. You may notice that the locations of nodes in this force-directed layout have nothing to do with where they're located on the globe.

Now each airport node has specific location coordinates embedded in their graph data, which will be useful when it comes to mapping them.

10.1.3   *Limitations to representing location as a property on a node*

In this case, it's the node that has a location, not the link. Although it's technically possible that LaGuardia airport could be moved to a different area of New York, for the purposes of this visualization it's fine to treat it as static. This works for most data sets, but there are instances where it's less helpful, such as when locations aren't fixed. Imagine you're tracking international shipping, and you want to map the relationships among goods, ports, and ships. The ports have a static location, but the ships are always moving, so their location depends on the date and time of analysis. The data model is straightforward—you'd just have multiple locations on each node tied to a date/time stamp—but the visualization technique is more difficult. One possible solution would be to bind a time bar like the one you saw in chapter 9 to map the location of the ships over specific windows of time and show just their graph when selected, where a graph could show that Ship 9 was in Port A on September 9. But no tool currently on the market can easily graph changing locations over time. The Gephi time bar is illustrated in figure 10.2 as a reminder.

Figure 10.2   The Gephi time bar—this could be used to visualize locations changing over time.

In addition, it's possible that the data model means that the location is a property of your links instead of your nodes. Imagine you're in charge of a sports league and you're interested in a graph of which teams will play each other over the course of a season. The nodes are the teams, and the games are the links, which have a date/time and a location. The location need not be the home field of one of the teams. Although this is a valid data model, you should avoid it if you want to visualize locations, because it's not possible to represent a link on a graph as a point on a map. Figure 10.3 shows an example.

Figure 10.3   The Carolina Panthers play the Denver Broncos in California. There's no good way to visualize the location of the game.

A line on a graph can't also be a point on a map. You can draw an element as either a line or a point on a map but not both. This presents a challenge when trying to draw this graph on a map, because the two nodes have a line between them. On a map, a line between North Carolina and Denver wouldn't go through Santa Clara; hence, the problem with trying to use a map to visualize this data.

10.2   Overlaying graphs on maps

Most graph data containing locations can be graphed on a map, however. As long as the nodes have static positions, as we discussed in the previous section, overlaying a graph on a map is really just another layout, but it's substantially different from the layouts we discussed in chapter 7. Whereas traditional layouts seek to place nodes to minimize clutter and maximize readability and understanding of the graph, a geographic layout is constrained on where items can go, because they have to be placed over their actual location on the map. Although a geographic layout creates another level of understanding by showing where nodes are physically located, it can result in charts that are more cluttered. I took the airline chart of the top 100 routes in the United States from figure 10.1 and overlaid the nodes on a map for figure 10.4.

The clutter can be a strength, though. A traditional graph visualization with a traditional force-directed layout would never reveal that these high-density routes cluster almost exclusively on the East Coast, Texas, and California. Another benefit of this

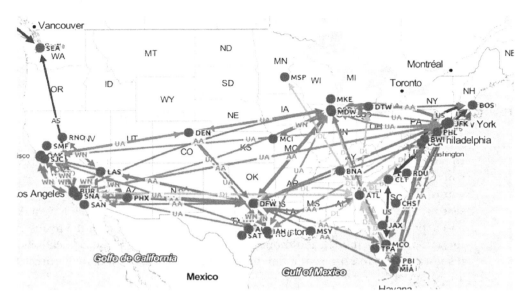

Figure 10.4   The airline route map superimposed on a map—some areas are very cluttered and others are empty.

map-based visualization is that the longer links actually mean something—in this case, the actual length of the flight between those two cities. By enabling the interactivity we discussed in chapter 6, specifically zooming and panning, users can zoom and pan into areas of interest. In figure 10.5, I zoomed in to focus only on the northeastern United States so we can see more detail, because in the national map, the data is too tightly packed to permit reading it properly.

At this level of detail, we can see clearly that the three New York airports have many of these routes. As mentioned earlier, unless you're an airport code buff, you may not realize that LGA, JFK, and EWR all serve New York until you superimpose them on a map. Figure 10.5 makes this clearer, though.

So when would this be added value? It's likely one of the uses of a graph like this would be to study the flow of passengers into and out of cities, not airports, so this could be important information if you're working at an airline and trying to judge capacity and plan new routes. An FAA official might use this graph to place new airports. But the links are crowded and hard to decipher. From Boston, there may be flights to New York and Philadelphia, but a link going to Washington, DC, may overlap those cities on a map. That's hard to tell, even at this zoom level. And there's another link back to the west whose endpoint is off the edge of the map, giving us no useful information. Graphs on maps can really only be used on very small data sets. Even this chart with 100 links is proving to be too busy for any useful analysis, so we'll have to filter the data to something more manageable.

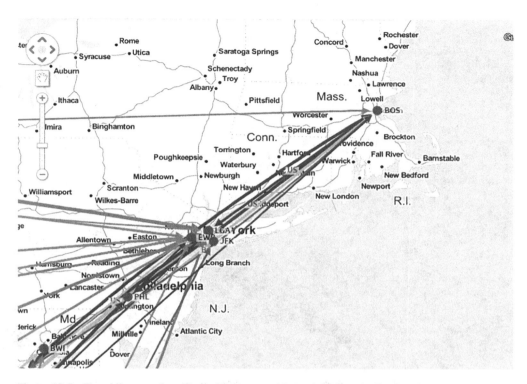

Figure 10.5 The airline map from figure 10.4, zoomed in to show just the Northeast

10.2.1 Filtering to subsets of the data

Too-large data sets are no good on maps because the relationships between nodes get cluttered. We discussed strategies for filtering to deal with large volumes of data in chapter 8, and some of them are as useful on maps as they are in force-directed graphs. Let's look at how to apply filters to large graphs of geographic data and make them more manageable.

First, let's go back to our original large data set of every domestic route in the U.S., containing approximately 14,000 city pairs, and show that on a map to demonstrate how too much data makes a graph useless. This is shown in figure 10.6.

It's no surprise that this is too much data to show all at once. But as we did with filtering on the traditional visualization, filtering on the map can also show results. Let's filter to show just Alaska Airlines; see figure 10.7.

This shows some interesting results. Alaska Airlines has hubs in Seattle and Portland, and nearly all their flights are from one of those two cities. Although they fly to the East Coast, nearly all their flights to the east are from their Pacific Northwest hubs. And the chart isn't particularly cluttered or difficult to read. So just like with force-directed charts, filtering can provide some value by allowing the user to geographically visualize smaller bits of data as needed instead of the entire data set all at once.

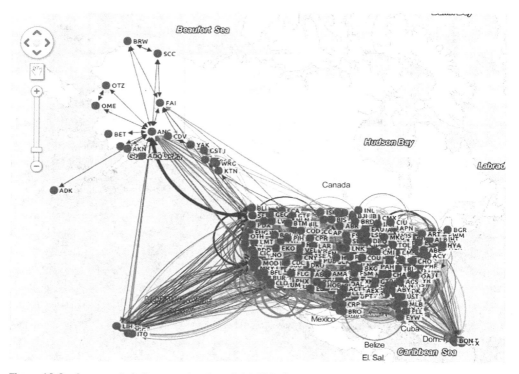

Figure 10.6   As expected, the map showing all 14,000 city pairs with airline service is useless. Only Alaska is clear, with few flights and a large land mass.

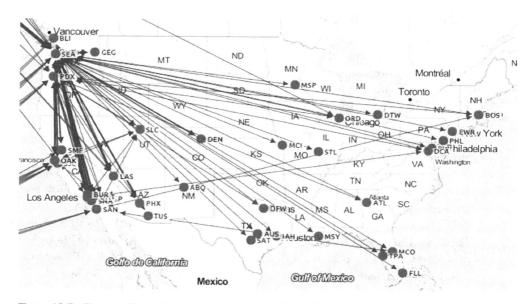

Figure 10.7   The map filtered to show only routes by Alaska Airlines

In chapter 8, we also discussed grouping nodes together to simplify visualizations. Although this can be applied to maps as well, it's not as straightforward as filtering is.

10.2.2 Combinations or grouping

Grouping together nodes that share a similar property to represent them as a single node on a chart can be a powerful tool for reducing clutter on a map just as it is for a chart, though there's no tool on the market to do this automatically. We could do this manually, however. Facebook has something similar already: the cities widget generates a map showing all your events or photos that have a location embedded in them and displays them as points on a map. Because you're likely to have a large number of check-ins and photos from a small number of areas (such as near your home or other frequently visited locations), Facebook has developed a clustering algorithm that automatically groups together items that are near to one another and replaces them with a dot that represents the entire group and is sized according to the number of items in that group. Figure 10.8 shows an example of a map of Facebook events.

This is not a graph because there are no links between the data elements, but it gives you a sense of how to do this yourself using the combination capability, and even at this level, you learn a lot about where this Facebook user spends their time.

Figure 10.8   A map of Facebook events, zoomed out to show the entire United States

Zooming in on the San Francisco Bay area shows more detail, because the large 65-event cluster breaks into smaller pieces to show exactly where photos or check-ins occurred, as you can see with figure 10.9.

Figure 10.9   A zoomed-in view of Facebook activity near San Francisco. Notice the clusters in San Francisco and San Jose but comparatively little activity around Oakland.

If we were to take our airline graph and replace the three New York–area airports with a single node representing all of metropolitan New York and showing flights into and out of the area, that would be an improvement. When the user zooms in on the map, it breaks out into the individual airports to make the individual data visible. Although there's no tool that does this grouping automatically, it can be done manually by using the combine methods in KeyLines or another tool. In figure 10.10, I show the three San Francisco airports combined into a single node and the two Los Angeles Airports combined as well.

Because no tool today does this automatically, you're stuck doing the combinations yourself. This means a three-step process:

1   Check the zoom level of the chart to know how close nodes need to be in space to be overlapping.
2   For each node, see if there are any others within the chosen radius.
3   Create a group of those nodes that fall within that radius.

Each time the user changes the zoom level on the chart, you'll need to run this process again.

So far, we've been talking generically about how to build and visualize graphs that contain location data. Now let's go through some examples on how to build them yourself.

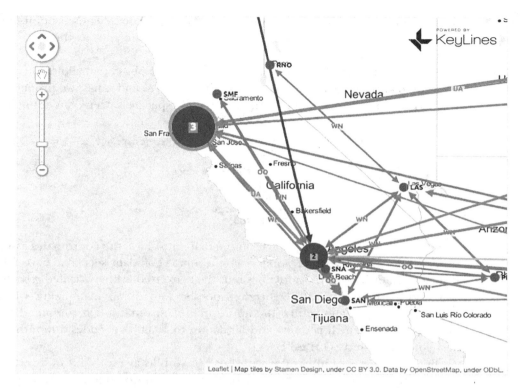

Figure 10.10   Using combinations to group together nearby nodes in KeyLines

10.3   *Building graphs on maps*

Thus far in the book, we've taken two approaches to various visualization features: showing Gephi for end users exploring their own data and KeyLines for people looking to build a graph visualization application themselves. Unfortunately, Gephi doesn't have any geographic capability, so I'll walk through how to build this capability in Key-Lines only. You can also use D3.js to create graphs on maps, and I'll show a D3 example in the appendix.

10.3.1   *Storing the data in the KeyLines object model*

For all the maps I've shown (except for the Facebook ones), I've used leaflet.js, which is an open source mapping library that does a lot of the hard work of showing maps within a web browser for you. This eliminates worrying about allowing zooming and panning, providing the right level of detail for the zoom level, and supporting mouse and gesture events. The Leaflet library itself doesn't provide the map tiles; those are downloaded from a map tiling server on demand. A bunch of commercial and free map tiling servers are available. In the previous examples, I used OpenStreetMap because it's free, but there are many other options that display satellite imagery, nighttime views, or even custom layers. Then it's a matter of overlaying the node icons as points and links as lines and ensuring that they snap to the appropriate spot as the user pans and zooms on the map.

With KeyLines, the JSON data model has a position object that allows you to assign a position to each node: pos is the name of the property, and it has two properties itself, lat and lng for numeric latitude and longitude, respectively. Here's an example:

```
{
  id: 'node1', t: 'label', type: 'node', u: 'person.png', x: 100, y: 150,
  pos: {
    lat: 52.2022,          ⟵      Must be in range
    lng: 0.1282    ⟵               -90 to 90
  }
}                          Must be in range
                           -180 to 180
```

Each node that you want to appear on the map must have the coordinates assigned. If they're missing, they won't appear on the map. For data sets that have addresses instead of coordinates, the addresses must be converted, which is called *geocoding*. You can find a number of free geocoders on the web of varying quality, which take addresses as input and return the appropriate coordinates. I recommend the Bing Maps geocoder, which is quick and allows up to 10,000 geocodes a month for free, and both REST and SOAP APIs.

Because KeyLines integrates with Leaflet, you'll have to build in a reference to leaflet.js in your HTML file that's hosting KeyLines; it would look something like the following:

```
<!DOCTYPE html>
<html>
  <head>
    <link rel='stylesheet' type='text/css' href='css/keylines.css'/>
    <link rel='stylesheet' type='text/css' href='css/leaflet.css'/>
    <script type="text/javascript" src="js/keylines.js"></script>
    <script type="text/javascript" src="js/leaflet.js"></script>

  </head>
```

Then, in the javascript container, there isn't a whole lot of code to write. The first step is to tell KeyLines where the map tiles are coming from, with a URL in the chart.map().options call. The Leaflet API documentation (http://leafletjs.com/reference.html#tilelayer-options) shows the detail of all the options available:

```
chart.map().options({
  tiles: {
    url: 'http://example.com/path/{z}/{x}/{y}.png',
    attribution: 'Attribution text',
    minZoom: 4,
    maxZoom: 12
  }
});
```

After that, you can toggle between viewing KeyLines items on a map with the `chart.map().show` and `chart.map().hide` functions. This allows you to see the data in both map mode and traditional mode in the same view.

Most but not all of the KeyLines functions detailed in chapters 5 and 6 are available in map mode also, like filtering, animating properties (though not location), and adding new data to the chart, and the API is the same. Running layouts will have no effect, as will trying to change the x and y properties or creating combinations.

10.3.2 *Building an example from the Hubway data*

Let's look at a couple of example data sets. In chapter 9, we looked at one scenario using data from the Boston Hubway program, which rents out bicycles from various kiosks in the cities of Boston and Cambridge. In figure 10.11, I've produced a chart using the data from figure 9.12. The source data is located at http://hubwaydatachallenge.org/.

In this example, the nodes are street corners where the Hubway program has kiosks where bikes can be rented or returned. If we manage the program, it's important to understand not just when bikes are rented but where the trips are taking place,

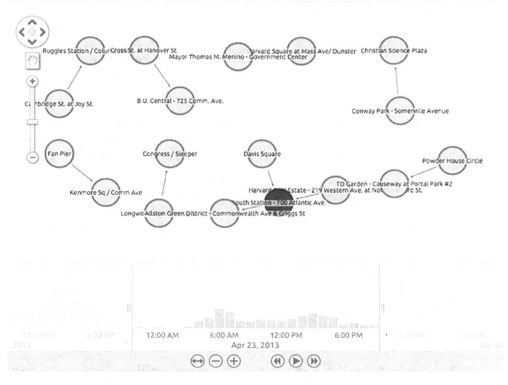

Figure 10.11 A graph using the same data as figure 9.12 showing the bicycles rented and returned at various stations around Boston

so it's also important to look at geography. Let's look at how to support this in Key-Lines. First, we have to find the geographic data in the source. Thankfully, with the Hubway data, it's already encoded in latitude and longitude, so we just need to encode that in our JSON:

```
{
id: 'B32006',
type: 'node',
t: 'Colleges of the Fenway',          Text that labels
c: 'rgb(0,128,173)'                   the node
pos: {                     Position
    lat: 42.340021         object
    lng: -71.100812
    }
}
```

Then we have to tell KeyLines which map tiles to use with the following code:

```
chart.map().options({
  tiles: {
  {
  id: 'tiles-cartodb-positron',
  name: 'CartoDB Positron',
  url: 'https://cartodb-basemaps-    {s}.global.ssl.fastly.net/light_all/{z}/
    {x}/{y}.png',
  attribution: 'CartoDB-Positron Map Tiles'    URL for CartoDB map
  }                                            tiles that we use for
}                                              the map
});
```

This tells KeyLines and leaflet.js where to download the tiles that form the background of the map. Then we want to bind two buttons to allow the user to switch between map and network modes. First, add the button to the HTML:

```
<input type="button" value="Map Mode" id="mapOn">
<input type="button" value="Network Mode" id="mapOff">
```

Once the buttons are on our page, we want to use the button click to change modes in our JavaScript:

```
$('#mapOn').click(function() {
  chart.map().show();
});
$('#mapOff').click(function() {
  chart.map().hide();
});
```

Now, clicking the Map Mode button on our page will switch the background of the chart to a map, using the tiles we've chosen, and run a layout to snap their positions to the actual locations of those stations; the example is shown in figure 10.12.

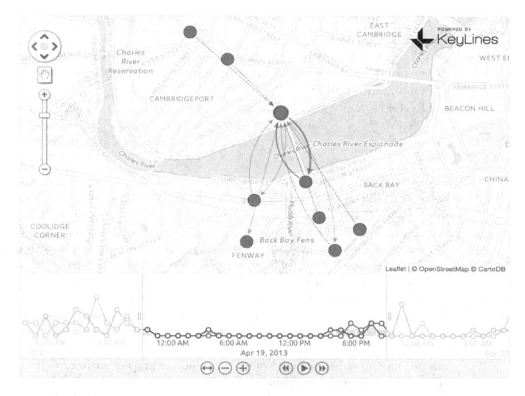

Figure 10.12 The network of rentals from the MIT station (on the North side of the river) on April 19, 2013, superimposed on a map

Say, for example, we're responsible for rebalancing the bikes—ensuring that not too many get taken from one station and returned to another to leave empty and over-flowing racks. In this case, we'd want to plan a van to go around to the stations and pick up bikes from the full racks and return them to the racks that have fewer bikes. To efficiently plan that route, we need to know the times of day when bikes are being rented and where the stations are, so that our van isn't needlessly crisscrossing the city. That's where a graph, superimposed on a map, could come in very handy.

10.4 Summary

In this chapter, you learned the following:

- One of the key reasons to visualize locations is to see which nodes are physically close to one another.
- There are many different ways of modeling geographic data, but current tools support only static positions on nodes.
- Superimposing graphs on maps eliminates the ability to run a layout to organize things, so be careful.

- For all but the smallest charts, it can be hard to see where links originate and terminate on a map.
- Filtering to smaller data sets is critical when working with geographic data.
- Gephi doesn't have this capability, and KeyLines has limited support by integrating with Leaflet.
- KeyLines data appears in the `pos` object under the `data` object for the node in the JSON.
- In KeyLines, `chart.map().hide()` and `chart.map().show()` get you into and out of map mode.

This concludes the main section of the book. We've discussed the principles of graph visualization and applied those principles to visualizations we've built using both Gephi and KeyLines. If you're interested in learning more about Gephi, it has a very good tutorial section at https://gephi.org/users/. In this book, I didn't go into much detail on the Gephi API, intending to focus more on the user interface, but if you're a software developer who wants to customize Gephi or build additional features, the place to start is its API, documented here: https://gephi.org/developers/.

KeyLines, not being an open source project, has less of a community surrounding it, but Cambridge Intelligence, the company that makes KeyLines, does make a wealth of information available on its YouTube channel, at https://www.youtube.com/user/cambridgeintel.

In the appendix, I apply some of the principles of graph visualization using another tool, D3.js, a well-used data visualization library. D3 is massive and deserves its own book; I can only scratch the surface here, but for a more in-depth discussion of D3 beyond just graphs, I recommend *D3.js in Action* by Elijah Meeks (Manning, 2015): www.manning.com/books/d3-js-in-action.

A tutorial on D3.js

This appendix covers

- A brief tutorial on D3.js, one of the popular open source JavaScript libraries for data visualization
- The graph visualization capability of the library
- Creating a simple graph visualization application using D3.js

D3 stands for *Data-Driven Documents* and is an extremely popular way to visualize data in a browser. It was designed by Mike Bostock in 2011 in an effort to separate the data layer of visualization from the visualization itself. This enables a programmer to allow for multiple visualizations of the same data on the same HTML page and facilitate interaction between them. This is not to say that D3 eliminates the need for a database—it's only intended to hold the data that you want to show on the page at that time, and there are memory and bandwidth considerations to how much data it's realistic to hold in a browser. D3.js has been used to create powerful and beautiful visualizations and is used in hundreds of web applications in many different industries. I encourage you to take a look at some of the examples at http://www.d3js.org.

A.1   *A brief introduction to D3.js*

D3.js is a JavaScript library that covers far more than graph visualizations. Browsing the samples at http://www.d3js.org reveals hundreds of powerful, interactive ways to explore data. I chose not to use D3 as the main tool for the body of this book for a couple of reasons. First, the D3 library is huge, and entire books have been written to cover its breadth. (I recommend *D3.js in Action* by Elijah Meeks; Manning, 2015.) Learning D3 at a level required to implement some of the advanced techniques described in the book would defeat the purpose of having a tutorial; additionally, I want to appeal to developers and non-developers alike. Second, D3 is a very low-level library. For example, creating a bar chart is not as simple as it might be in Excel—defining the axes, labels, and colors and pointing the chart at the data. Instead, you must program the drawing of the individual rectangles representing the bars, position them, and define the scale and layout with some specific drawing code. Although this provides ultimate flexibility in how you want your bar chart to look, it requires a lot of code. Nonetheless, D3 is very popular for creating graph visualizations and it has some built-in capability for dealing with graph data. What I show in this appendix is how to use D3 to create graph visualizations, and I'll walk through a brief tutorial with some sample data.

A.1.1   *Selectors*

The fundamental feature of D3 is the use of selectors. To do virtually anything using D3, you have to select various elements in the DOM (Document Object Model) and modify them. A *selection* is a list of those DOM elements that match a defined pattern that you can edit *en masse*. These are typically traditional DOM elements like text paragraphs or DIV elements:

```
selection = d3.selectAll("div.dog");
```

This will select all DIV elements on the page with a class of dog. You can now work with that selection object with a number of built-in functions that we'll go over in the tutorial. You can also use d3.select, which returns only the first item that matches the criterion, but selectAll is more useful.

A.1.2   *Data formats*

D3 can accept data in a number of different formats: JSON, CSV, HTML, XML, or text. Regardless of your original data source, there's usually some way to obtain the data and pass it to the browser in one of these formats, and I talk about how to translate data into nodes and links in chapter 4. For graphs, CSV or JSON makes the most sense, because you can assemble lists of nodes and edges with the properties that you want to show similar to the way it works in KeyLines. One important difference is that, although KeyLines publishes the JSON format in which your data has to be formatted for correct drawing, with node sizes, colors, and edge widths each giving specifically named properties, D3 allows you to set those visual properties from the CSS on the

HTML page itself. It's generally easiest to sit this alongside the HTML and JavaScript files. You use the d3.json or d3.csv function to load the data into the visualization. You'll see an example of this in section A.2.

A.1.3 SVG drawing

A key feature of D3 is that it draws the graph on the web page using SVG (Scalable Vector Graphics). Although an HTML5 Canvas mode and a WebGL mode do exist, they aren't yet easily supported for the graph capability. SVG has slightly lower performance than either Canvas or WebGL, but you'll still see smooth animations up to a few hundred nodes on a chart. You can use the selectors described in section A.1.1 to get a selection containing the DOM element that you want to be the visualization, and then use the d3.append function to change it to an svg tag with the size attributes that you want to use:

```
var svg = d3.select("body").append("svg")
    .attr("width", 800)
    .attr("height", 800);
```

This will take the body tag and add a square svg tag with height and width attributes set to 800 pixels inside it. But of course, there's nothing in the visualization yet. You need to add a drawing:

```
var circleElement = d3.select("svg").append("circle")
    .attr("r", 20)
    .attr("cx", 100)
    .attr("cy", 100)
    .style("fill", "red");
```

This will create a red circle element on your SVG canvas with a radius of 10, located 100 pixels from the top-left corner of the canvas, as shown in figure A.1.

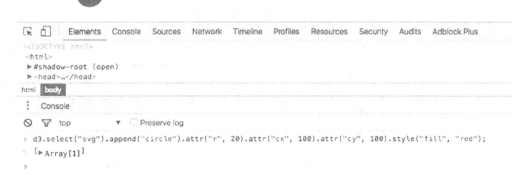

Figure A.1   A lonely red circle on our SVG canvas, created from the Chrome console

A.1.4   *Interactivity*

Before we get to graphs, one more important feature of D3 is the ability to create interactivity, such as trapping mouse clicks, hovers, and drags, and to bind behavior to that user action. Because the drawing elements are HTML DOM elements, the typical HTML mouse events are supported: clicks, mouseovers, mouseouts, and so on. This is done with the .on() function on the selection object. So if we take the circleElement object from earlier, we can change the color when the mouse hovers over the object with the following code:

```
var circleElement.on("mouseover", changeColor);

circleElement.on("mouseout", changeColorBack);
function changeColor(d) {
    circleElement.style("fill", "blue");
}
function changeColorBack(d) {
    circleElement.style("fill", "red");
}
```

Runs the changeColor function when the mouse hovers over the circle

When the mouse pointer leaves the color, changes the color back

The d variable represents the data bound to the circle element; this can be useful if we want to check the data to determine how to change an item, but we're ignoring this for now.

This code instantaneously changes the color of the circle, but you saw in chapter 5 that it can often be useful to animate changes to visualizations, so for that we can use the transition() function:

```
function changeColor(d) {
        circleElement.transition().duration(500).attr("r", 50);
}
```

This will grow the radius of the circle to 50 pixels over the course of a half-second (500 milliseconds).

A.1.5   *Graphs in D3*

D3 offers many ways to represent nodes and links, but we'll focus on node-link diagrams as we do for much of this book. In D3, a graph visualization isn't anything special; it's just a collection of the primitive drawing elements that represent the nodes and links. Links are almost always SVG lines, but nodes can be circles, rectangles, or images. Although we'll stick with circles in this chapter to keep the code simple, keep in mind that node icons can often be useful, as mentioned in chapter 5.

You could build a node-link diagram from your data by drawing a circle for each node and a line between each node representing the relationship between them, but that's a lot of work. You'd also have to position the nodes manually using the CX and CY attributes, which is practically not much better than drawing a graph by hand. Thankfully, the d3.forceSimulation() namespace offers some additional graph-drawing features automatically. It implements the force-directed layout that we discussed in chapter 7 to automatically position the nodes to make the chart more readable and place the well-connected nodes in the center. First, you need to give the layout the data, which is an array of the nodes and links that you want to show, similar to the way KeyLines accepts the data. The `forceSimulation` object requires two arrays be passed to `forceSimulation.nodes([array])` and `forceSimulation.links([array])`. The nodes array can have any properties that you find useful (which can dictate node size, color, icon, and the like), except for a few reserved properties:

- `index`—Uniquely defines the node
- `x`—The *x* coordinate of the current node position
- `y`—The *y* coordinate of the current node position
- `vx`—The velocity of the node in the x direction
- `vy`—The velocity of the node in the y direction
- `fx`—Determines whether the node is locked in position on the x-axis
- `fy`—Determines whether the node is locked in position on the y-axis
- `weight`—The node weight; the number of associated links

With D3 version 4, there's also a unique ID property like with KeyLines, so if an object appears twice in your list, it will have two duplicate nodes in the visualization. Any de-duplication will have to happen before you create the node list.

The array passed to links does require specific properties representing the source and destination (the two nodes representing the endpoints) of the links. The source and destination use the 0-based index of that node's position in the array, so `{"source":1,"target":0,}` would represent a link from the second entry in the node array to the first entry. You can also set the `source` and `target` properties to the ID string of the nodes as opposed to the indexes.

You can tweak the force-directed layout by defining custom forces on each node—this is a new feature from D3 version 3, which allowed you to edit constants but not define custom force functions. This isn't for the faint of heart, and I rarely find straying far from the defaults to be helpful, but following are a few to play with:

```
d3.forceSimulation.force("charge", d3.forceManyBody())
```

The `forceManyBody` namespace allows you to customize the strength of the pull between nodes similar to gravity on the chart. A higher number means the nodes will be pulled together more strongly and a negative number means the nodes will be pushed away from each other.

```
.force("center"), d3.forceCenter()
```

This represents the center of the chart that the nodes are being pulled toward. By default this is `(0,0)`, but you may want a different center.

```
.force("link", d3.forceLink())
```

This is new for D3 version 4. Instead of setting an attractive force for links globally, you can customize it on a per-link basis. This means that you can pass an array of link IDs and set a different attractive force for each one.

The simulation starts automatically and runs the layout continuously until `simula-tion.stop` is called. The event "tick" allows you to make changes to the chart with each iteration of the force-directed layout.

This is a lot to digest, so in the next section, we'll create a node-link diagram from scratch using D3 and annotate each section of the code.

A.2   *Building a graph in D3.js*

Now that we've gone over some of the basics of how to create elements using D3 and some of the features of the force-directed layout, you'll see how it all comes together by building a sample visualization. We'll return to the Abramoff chart we worked with in chapters 5–7 so that you can see the difference in the way you work with the data and design in D3 versus Gephi or KeyLines. We'll start with the HTML setting up the chart. As you can see, it's quite minimal—we'll use D3 and JavaScript to build our visualization. Our example will have only the chart on it, not any additional HTML, but you'll definitely want more on your page:

```
<!DOCTYPE html>
<meta charset="utf-8">
<style>

.node {
  stroke: #fff;
  stroke-width: 1px;
}

.link {
  stroke: #fff;
}

</style>
<body>
<script src="//d3js.org/d3.v4.min.js"></script>
<script src="d3jsExample.js"></script>
```

> CSS syntax that defines the visual properties of the nodes and links, in this case, color and width. We'll bundle it into the HTML for now, but in a true application you'd have a separate CSS file.

> The reference to the minified D3 library from d3js

You'll notice that we reference a separate JavaScript file called d3jsExample.js—this will be our integration code that adds the chart to the page:

```
var simulation = d3.forceSimulation()
    .force("link", d3.forceLink().id(function(d) { return d.index; }))
    .force("charge", d3.forceManyBody())
    .force("center", d3.forceCenter(width / 2, height / 2);

var svg = d3.select("body").append("svg")
    .attr("width", 800)
    .attr("height", 800);

d3.json("abramoffChart.json", function(error, graph) {

    simulation
        .nodes(graph.nodes)
        .links(graph.links)
        .start();
```

> Creates the D3 force object and sets the size and properties of the layout

> Adds these objects to the SVG canvas

> Loads the Abramoff chart data in a separate JSON file

> Sets the nodes and links properties to the arrays found in the JSON

Sets the properties of the link object in the JSON to the data property in D3 so that we can use it later

```
var link = svg.selectAll(".link")
    .data(graph.links)
    .enter().append("line")
    .attr("class", "link")
    .style("stroke-width", function(d) { return
    Math.Pow(d.value, 0.25); });

var node = svg.selectAll(".node")
    .data(graph.nodes)
    .enter().append("circle")
    .attr("class", "node")
    .attr("r", 10)
    .style("fill", function(d)
        { if (d.guilty) {
          return "red";}
          if (d.indicted) {
           return "orange";}
           return "yellow"; })
    .call(d3.drag()
        .on("start", dragstarted)
        .on("drag", dragged)
        .on("end", dragended));

node.append("title")
    .text(function(d) { return d.name; });

simulation
     .nodes(graph.nodes)
     .on("tick", ticked);

    simulation.force("link")
      .links(graph.links);

function ticked() {
   link.attr("x1", function(d) { return d.source.x; })
       .attr("y1", function(d) { return d.source.y; })
       .attr("x2", function(d) { return d.target.x; })
       .attr("y2", function(d) { return d.target.y; });

   node.attr("cx", function(d) { return d.x; })
       .attr("cy", function(d) { return d.y; });
  });
});

function dragstarted(d) {

  d.fx = d.x;
  d.fy = d.y;
}

function dragged(d) {
  d.fx = d3.event.x;
  d.fy = d3.event.y;
}

function dragended(d) {

  d.fx = null;
  d.fy = null;
}
```

Adds a line for each link in the data

Sets the link width to the fourth root of the dollar amount to scale things appropriately

Does the same thing with the nodes

Sets the fill color to whether the indicted or guilty property is in our data

Allows the user to drag the nodes around with the mouse

Sets the title property to the name of the node in the data

Attaches a function to each tick of the force-directed layout

Ticked function moves the nodes to where the forces say they should be

Sets the link width to the fourth root of the dollar amount to scale things appropriately

Moves the nodes when the user drags them around

Once the simulation function is called, the layout will run continuously and call the function attached to tick continuously. In the previous code sample, we loaded abramoff-Chart.json, which is the JSON file containing our data. This is shown next, and it comprises two arrays, one of nodes and one of links:

```json
{
  "nodes":[
    {"name":"Brent R. Wilkes","indicted":false, "guilty":false},
    {"name":"Ed Buckham","indicted":false, "guilty": false},
    {"name":"Jack Abramoff","indicted":true, "guilty": true},
    {"name":"Rep. Tom Delay","indicted":true, "guilty": false},
    {"name":"Rep. Duncan Hunter","indicted":false, "guilty": false},
    {"name":"Rep. John T. Doolittle","indicted":false, "guilty": false},
    {"name":"Former Rep. Bill Lowery","indicted":false, "guilty": false},
    {"name":"Rep. Jerry Lewis","indicted":false, "guilty": false},
    {"name":"Mitchell J. Wade","indicted":true, "guilty": true},
    {"name":"Randy Duke Cunningham","indicted":true, "guilty":true},
    {"name":"Rep. Virgil H. Goode Jr","indicted":false, "guilty":false},
    {"name":"Brant G. (Nine Fingers) Bassett","indicted":false,
     "guilty":false},
    {"name":"Kyle Dusty Goggo","indicted":false, "guilty":false},
    {"name":"Shirlington Limousine","indicted":false, "guilty":false}
    ],
  "links":[
    {"source":0,"target":1,"value":1},
    {"source":0,"target":3,"value":1},
    {"source":0,"target":4,"value":18200},
    {"source":0,"target":5,"value":85000},
    {"source":0,"target":6,"value":160000},
    {"source":0,"target":7,"value":60000},
    {"source":0,"target":8,"value":1},
    {"source":0,"target":9,"value":1},
    {"source":0,"target":11,"value":5000},
    {"source":0,"target":12,"value":1},
    {"source":0,"target":13,"value":1},
    {"source":1,"target":2,"value":1},
    {"source":1,"target":3,"value":1},
    {"source":2,"target":5,"value":1},
    {"source":11,"target":12,"value":1},
    {"source":12,"target":13,"value":1},
    {"source":8,"target":9,"value":1000000},
    {"source":10,"target":8,"value":1},
  ]
}
```

The list of nodes has as properties the names of the individuals, whether they have been indicted, and whether they had been found guilty. You can use whatever properties you decide, because the JavaScript will handle converting those to visual properties. In this case, we'll use whether the person has been indicted or found guilty to control the color of the node. On the array of links, we have the required source and target properties, but we've also included a value property, which is the dollar amount of campaign contributions that has changed hands between the individuals. In the case where the relationship doesn't include a cash contribution, I set the value to 1. The result is shown in figure A.2.

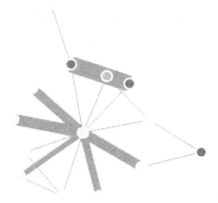

Figure A.2 A simple link chart in D3 showing the Abramoff chart we used in chapters 6 and 7. Notice that we're binding the link width to the value of the campaign contributions and the node color to the `indicted` and `guilty` properties.

By setting the `title` property of the nodes, D3 will automatically create a tooltip on the mouse hover to give us the name of the person, but in this case, because it's a small chart, we may want to see the labels on the chart itself. A small modification to the JavaScript supports this. Instead of creating circle nodes directly on the canvas, we need to create group nodes and add both a label and a circle to each group:

```
var gnodes = svg.selectAll('g.gnode')          ◁─┐ gnode is now
    .data(graph.nodes)                             │ group node
    .enter()
    .append('g')
    .classed('gnode', true);

  var node = gnodes.append('circle')           ◁─┐ Attaches a circle
    .data(graph.nodes)                             │ to each group
    .attr("class", "node")
    .attr("r", 5)
    .style("fill", function(d)
        {
        if (d.guilty) {
        return 'red';}
        else if (d.indicted) {
        return 'orange';}
        return 'yellow'; })
                                                │ Attaches a text
    .call(force.drag);                          │ label to each
  gnodes.append("text")               ◁─┘ group
    .attr("dx", 12)
    .attr("dy", ".35em")
    .text(function(d) { return d.name });

gnodes.attr("cx", function(d) { return d.x; })
    .attr("cy", function(d) { return d.y; })
```

```
.attr("transform", function(d)
    { return "translate(" + d.x + "," + d.y + ")"; });
```
◁─┤ **Places the label to the right of the circle**

The name of the item is now a text primitive along with the circle, placed to the right of the circle on the chart, as shown in figure A.3.

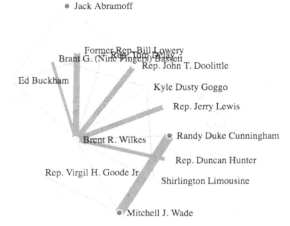

Figure A.3   The Abramoff chart in D3 with labels attached to the nodes. Note that D3 doesn't automatically take the length of the label into account when running the layout, so some of the text overlays other labels.

This was a brief introduction to using D3 for graph visualization. Although it's a low-level library, requiring you to work with drawing primitives directly, it can be incredibly powerful for creating custom interactions, especially between different visualizations of the same data.

A.3   Summary

In this appendix, you learned the following:

- D3 is a powerful library for creating custom, interactive visualizations of all sorts, not just graph visualizations.
- It's a low-level library, allowing you great flexibility in designing applications but requiring lots of source code.
- D3 accepts data in a number of different formats, including JSON, XML, and CSV.
- The force layout allows you to pass arrays of nodes and links and will automatically run a force-directed layout on the items.
- A more in-depth treatment of D3 can be found online at d3js.org and in the book *D3.js in Action.*

Neo4j in Action
by Aleksa Vukotic and Nicki Watt with Tareq Abe-
    drabbo, Dominic Fox, and Jonas Partner

ISBN: 9781617290763
304 pages
$44.99
December 2014

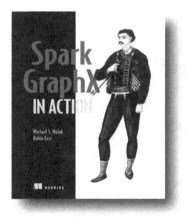

Spark GraphX in Action
by Michael S. Malak and Robin East

ISBN: 9781617292521
280 pages
$49.99
June 2016

Spark in Action
by Petar Zečević and Marko Bonaći

ISBN: 9781617292606
472 pages
$49.99
November 2016

For ordering information go to www.manning.com

MORE TITLES FROM MANNING

Practical Data Science with R
by Nina Zumel and John Mount

  ISBN: 9781617291562
  416 pages
  $49.99
  March 2014

Geoprocessing with Python
by Chris Garrard

  ISBN: 9781617292149
  360 pages
  $49.99
  May 2016

D3.js in Action
by Elijah Meeks

  ISBN: 9781617292118
  352 pages
  $44.99
  February 2015

For ordering information go to www.manning.com